Heroes of Jewish History

VOLUME TWO

JOSHUA TO JEREMIAH

THE LAND OF ISRAEL

HEROES OF
JEWISH HISTORY

VOLUME TWO

From Joshua to Jeremiah

WITH EXERCISES,
PROJECTS AND GAMES

By

MORDECAI H. LEWITTES

Illustrations by
CHARLES E. PONT

HEBREW PUBLISHING COMPANY
NEW YORK

TO DON JORDAN

AND TO THOSE WHO LOVE TO HEAR
THE TALES
OF THE HEROES OF OLD

PRINTED AND BOUND IN U.S.A. BY
MONTAUK BOOK MANUFACTURING CO., INC., NEW YORK

Preface

This book is a sequel to Volume I which covered the Biblical period from Abraham to Moses.

As in the first volume the author utilized the following principles and methods:

1. *Lives of the Heroes*—Nothing is more absorbing to the young reader than an exciting tale centering around the life of a great leader. Through the pages of Biblical history march the commanding figures of prophets, kings and popular heroes.

2. *Selection*—Jewish history suffers from an embarrassment of riches. The youthful student is often confused by the many names with which he is confronted. Through proper selection and emphasis each leader included can become a vivid, clearly-defined personality. It is for this reason that a chapter has been devoted to Samson but none to Jephthah. Important though they are, Amos and Hosea are omitted but four chapters are devoted to Isaiah and Jeremiah.

3. *Style*—The stories are told simply and dramatically. The author feels that it is most important not to talk down to the pupil. The language used, however, must be readily comprehended.

4. *Organization*—The book is based on six main units. Each unit contains several chapters which, in turn, are

divided into small, convenient sections. This division facilitates the planning of individual lessons as well as larger units.

5. *Holidays and Jewish Values*—Holidays and other Jewish values become more significant if properly emphasized in a history text. Examples are Ruth and Shavuot, Elijah and Passover, Jonah and Yom Kippur, Isaiah and the ideal of peace.

6. *Research*—The findings of archaeology and research are woven into the text. The child thus learns about Solomon's mines, the spread of the alphabet, the Siloam inscription etc.

7. *Projects*—"We learn to do by doing" has become axiomatic. Many worthwhile projects and activities are suggested.

8. *Exercises*—These will aid in mastery of the material studied.

9. *Pedagogic Aids*—Systematic reviews and tests, a pronunciation guide, maps and illustrations—all are valuable aids to student and teacher. The puzzles and games provide an opportunity for fun and relaxation.

10. *Format*—The attractive format of the book will stimulate a desire in the pupil to read and to study.

Judaism has been called a historical religion. Through a study of Jewish history the pupil will gain an insight into the teachings of our great religious leaders as well as knowledge concerning our past.

Contents

PAGE

UNIT ONE

Into the Promised Land

1. Jericho   17
2. Be Strong and of Good Courage!   28
3. Joshua—First In Peace   36

UNIT TWO

The Judges

4. Deborah—The Woman Who Freed Israel   47
5. Gideon—The Judge Who Would Not Be King   56
6. The Story of Ruth   65
7. Samson and the Philistines   75

UNIT THREE

The Beginning of the Kingdom

8. Samuel   89
9. Saul—Israel's First King   99
10. David, the Shepherd Hero   110
11. Saul and David   120

UNIT FOUR

King David and King Solomon

12. David—King of Israel   135

13. David and the Prophet Nathan   144
14. "My Son, Absalom!"   152
15. An Understanding Heart   161
16. Wise King Solomon   169

UNIT FIVE

The Divided Kingdom

17. The Revolt of the Ten Tribes of Israel   187
18. Elijah the Prophet   195
19. Jonah and the Message of Forgiveness   209

UNIT SIX

The Prophets of Judah

20. Isaiah   221
21. Isaiah's Prophecy of Peace   228
22. Jeremiah—the Prophet of Sorrow   241
23. Destruction and New Hope   252

Glossary   267

Illustrations

	PAGE
The Land of Israel	*Frontispiece*
Joshua Before the Walls of Jericho	23
The Twelve Tribes of Israel	39
The Defeat of Sisera	53
Ruth in the Fields of Bethlehem	69
Samson Carrying Away the Gates of Gaza	81
David the Shepherd	113
Solomon Dedicating the Temple	173
Elijah Accuses Ahab	197
Jonah: "I Am a Hebrew"	211
The Vision of Isaiah: "And they shall beat their swords into plowshares"	237

TO THE STUDENT

Have you ever heard somebody say, "I am proud to be a Jew"? When we hear the story of our heroes and learn about the great teachings of our people, we begin to understand why we are proud to be Jews.

In the first book we read about Abraham, the father of the Hebrew people. He taught his family not to worship idols, but to believe in one God.

Obeying God's command, Abraham wandered into Canaan, the promised land. There he made a *brith* or covenant with God.

"Let your chidren follow My laws of truth and of kindness," said God, "and I will give them the land of Canaan as an inheritance."

Isaac and Jacob renewed this covenant with God. Jacob, who was also called Israel, became the ancestor of the 12 tribes of Israel. His beloved son, Joseph, who was sold as a slave rose to the rank of prime minister of Egypt, and saved the country from famine. Joseph's father and brothers joined him in Egypt becoming shepherds in a section called Goshen.

Many years later, a new Pharaoh made slaves of the children of Israel. Moses and Aaron were sent as messengers by God to free the slaves. After the crossing of the Red Sea, Moses led the children of Israel to Mount Sinai where

they received the 10 commandments. These commandments teach us to believe in one God, to honor our parents,
to rest on the Sabbath, not to steal or to kill.

For forty years Moses led the children of Israel through
the desert. Our holidays remind us of these great events.
Passover is a reminder of the freeing of the Israelites from
slavery. On Shavuot we celebrate the granting of the 10
commandments at Sinai. The holiday of Sukkot helps us
to remember how the children of Israel wandered through
the desert for 40 years.

At last the Israelites were ready to enter the promised
land. Before his death Moses appointed Joshua as leader,
and warned the people to obey the laws of God.

How did Joshua lead the children of Israel into Canaan?
What new leaders arose in time of trouble? How did the
kings unite the 12 tribes? What did the prophets teach
the people?

Book II will help us to learn the answers to these questions. We shall read many exciting stories about the heroes
of Jewish history, and shall learn about the great teachings
of the Bible.

UNIT ONE

Into the Promised Land

CHAPTER I

JERICHO

1. JOSHUA TAKES COMMAND

AFTER the death of Moses, God spoke to Joshua saying: "Lead the children of Israel over the Jordan River into the land of Canaan. Be strong and of good courage for I shall be with you. Only remember to observe the laws which I have given unto Moses."

Joshua commanded the officers to warn the people to prepare food for the journey.

The officers moved throughout the camp shouting, "Get ready to break up camp! In a few more days we shall cross the Jordan River!"

There was great excitement indeed in the camp. This was the day for which the children of Israel had waited for forty years. Those who had been slaves in Egypt had died in the desert. But a new generation had grown up loving freedom.

"Long live Joshua!" the brave soldiers shouted. "We will follow him to victory!"

"How different is the spirit of the children of Israel today from what it was 40 years ago", said Joshua with a smile. "God is with us and He will surely keep His promise. For God promised Canaan unto Abraham, Isaac and Jacob."

2½ tribes had already received land east of the Jordan. Joshua called the leaders of these tribes to him and said: "You were the first to receive land for yourselves and for your wives and children. Remember, however, that you swore to march with the rest of Israel over the Jordan until the land has been conquered."

"Well do we remember", said the leaders of the tribes of Reuben, Gad and half the tribe of Manasseh. "We will surely keep our word. Our families will live in the cities which we have built east of the Jordan. When Canaan has been conquered then we shall return to our homes."

Joshua was pleased with their reply. He knew he could now proceed with his plans.

Joshua picked two brave soldiers for a dangerous mission.

"Cross the Jordan," said Joshua, "and enter the city of Jericho. Find out how strong the city is, and whether we shall be able to conquer the city easily. You may go disguised as merchants."

"We will do our best," replied the soldiers.

2. THE TWO SPIES

The two soldiers quickly crossed the Jordan and then made their way to the city of Jericho. Around the city was a large wall. Through the gate in the wall many people entered the city. Some were farmers who had come to sell their fruits. Others were merchants who bought and sold garments and shoes and pottery and little household idols.

"Maybe they won't notice us," said one of the spies. "We are dressed like the other merchants."

The two spies marched quickly through the gate of the city behind a traveler riding on the back of a donkey. Nobody stopped them.

The spies walked through the streets of Jericho. They observed where the wall was strongest and where it was weakest. In the market-place they listened to the conversations, and overheard several people speak with alarm of the approaching Israelites.

Later they went to an inn not far from the city-gate.

The house was owned by a woman named Rahab. After they had eaten, Rahab approached the two spies and said, "Are you not Israelites? I have watched you closely."

The spies were silent.

"I know you are Israelites. How can I help you? I know God is with you, and I am eager to help."

The spies believed Rahab, and admitted who they were.

"We have heard of your great leaders," said Rahab, "and our hearts melt with fear. I shall help you in whatever way I can. Only promise that you will not harm me or my family."

"You will be treated with kindness," replied the spies.

"Quickly come with me," said Rahab. She led them to the flat roof of her house where stalks of flax were drying.

"Several of my guests are spies for the king," Rahab whispered. "You have surely been seen. Hide beneath the flax, and later I shall come to help you escape."

It was not a minute too soon. There were loud knocks on the door.

"Rahab, Rahab, open! Israelite spies have been seen in your house."

Rahab opened the door and the king's guards entered.

"Where are the two Israelites?" they demanded.

"There were two strangers here," replied Rahab, "but I did not know who they were. They left at twilight just before the closing of the gates of the city. Hurry after them. They could not have gone very far."

The Jericho soldiers searched for the spies as far as the Jordan River, but they found nobody.

Rahab then went to the roof where the spies were hiding. "My house is next to the wall of the city. The roof rests on the wall. By means of this cord I can let you down over the side of the wall."

In her hand, Rahab held a scarlet cord.

"Hide in the mountains for three days," continued Rahab. "Then you can safely cross the Jordan."

"We owe our lives to you," said one of the spies. "Place this scarlet cord in the window of your house. When the Israelites see this cord they will deal kindly with you and your family."

Rahab lowered the spies over the wall by means of the rope.

The spies escaped from Jericho and hid in the mountains for three days. Meanwhile, their pursuers returned to Jericho and reported to the king that the spies could nowhere be found.

After three days the spies crossed the Jordan in safety.

"What have you seen?" asked Joshua when the spies were brought before him.

"Jericho is a strong walled city," replied the spies, "but the hearts of the people melt with fear, for they know that they cannot fight against Israel."

3. ACROSS THE JORDAN

At last came the order: "Forward! Across the Jordan!"

The ark of God in which were the two tablets of the law led the way. The priests carrying the ark were the first to wade into the river. Behind them came the entire camp of the children of Israel.

The Jordan is a rapid river. Its waters descend quickly from rock to rock. In Hebrew it is called *Ha-Yarden* which means "the descender" for the Jordan drops from the mountain tops in the north to the Dead Sea, the lowest spot on the face of the earth.

The Israelites crossed at one of the fords of the river, a shallow spot where the water is not too deep.

On the day that Joshua led the people across the Jordan, the mighty river became almost a trickle. Beneath them the children of Israel could see the sand of the river bed. It was almost like the day when they had crossed the Red Sea on dry land.

"As a memorial of this great day," said Joshua, "let us

take twelve stones from the river bed. These stones we shall set up as a monument to remind us of the crossing of the Jordan."

The Israelites set up camp at a place called Gilgal in the plains of Jericho. A short distance away the palm trees of Jericho swayed gently in the wind.

It was at Gilgal that the Israelites observed the first Passover ever to be celebrated on the soil of the Land of Israel.

The children of Israel remembered the words of the first commandment: "I am the Lord thy God who brought thee out of the land of Egypt out of the house of bondage."

As they ate the *matzah* or unleavened bread they were reminded of how their fathers had quickly baked unleavened bread in their haste to leave Egypt.

On this day they had been freed from slavery, and now God had kept His promise and had brought them into the promised land.

It was at Gilgal, too, that the people ate for the first time the fruits of the new land. The manna, which had kept them alive in the desert, did not fall after they crossed the Jordan.

4. THE FALL OF JERICHO

Now Joshua made plans for the conquest of Jericho. The king of Jericho ordered the gate of the city to be closed so that nobody could enter or leave. On the walls of the city the archers stood guard, ready to defend the city against the attackers.

JOSHUA BEFORE THE WALLS OF JERICHO

"When you enter the city," warned Joshua, "remember to deal kindly with Rahab and with all who are in her house. By the scarlet cord in her window you will recognize her house. Let nobody take for himself of the gold or silver or possessions that are in Jericho. Whatever you capture shall be given to the treasury of the Lord."

And God said to Joshua, "Let the army of Israel go around the walls of Jericho once each day for six days. Behind the soldiers seven priests will march carrying rams' horns. Each priest will blow on the *shofar* as he marches around the city, but the soldiers must remain silent. The priests will be followed by the ark of God.

"On the seventh day, the people will rise early in the morning. On this day they will march around the wall seven times. Then the priests will blow a long blast on the rams' horns. This will be a signal for the people to shout with a great shout. And the wall of the city will fall down flat."

Joshua gave these commands unto the children of Israel. For six days the soldiers marched around Jericho. Behind the army were seven priests blowing on rams' horns. Last came the ark of God.

On the wall of Jericho the archers watched in wonder. What did this mean? They knew that they could not attack the Israelites on the open plain. But when would the children of Israel try to storm the wall? They watched as the soldiers marched silently around the city each day and the hearts of the archers melted with fear.

On the seventh day, after marching around the wall seven times, the priests blew a long blast on the *shofar*.

"Shout," Joshua commanded, "for the Lord has given you the city."

A mighty shout went up from the Israelite army. Then wonder of wonders, the walls of Jericho fell down flat. An earthquake had caused the walls to come tumbling down.

The children of Israel rushed into Jericho and soon conquered the frightened city. Rahab and her family were saved as the spies had promised.

The children of Israel had won their first battle on the soil of Canaan.

The world has never forgotten this great battle. To this very day people sing joyously:

"Joshua fought the battle of Jericho
And the walls came tumbling down!"

EXERCISES

I. Fill in the missing name. (Review the section called "To the Student", pages 13 to 14.)

1. _____ is the father of the Hebrew people.
2. God promised the land of _____ to the Hebrew people.
3. _____ renewed the covenant that God had made with Abraham.
4. _____, or Israel, is the father of the 12 tribes.
5. _____ became prime minister of Egypt.
6. Pharaoh, ruler of _____, made slaves of the children of Israel.
7. _____ freed the children of Israel from slavery.
8. The holiday of _____ reminds us of the exodus from Egypt.

9. The holiday of _____ reminds us of the granting of the ten commandments.

10. The holiday of _____ reminds us of the booths which the Israelites built when they wandered in the desert.

II. Choose the correct word or name. (Review section 1, pages 17 to 18.)

1. God said to _____, "Lead the children of Israel into Canaan." (Joshua, Moses)

2. The officers warned the people, "Get ready to cross the _____." (Euphrates, Jordan)

3. The children of Israel had wandered in the desert for _____ years. (thirty, forty)

4. The tribe of Reuben received land _____ of the Jordan. (east, west)

5. Joshua sent two spies to _____. (Jericho, Jerusalem)

III. How? (Review section 2, pages 18 to 21.)

1. How did the spies gain entrance to Jericho?

2. How did Rahab hide the spies on the roof?

3. How did Rahab help the spies to escape from Jericho?

4. How did the spies reach the Jordan safely?

5. How would the children of Israel recognize Rahab's house?

IV. Tell briefly about each of the following. (Review sections 3 and 4, pages 21 to 25.)

1. The Jordan

2. Crossing into Canaan

3. The first Passover on the soil of Canaan

4. Joshua's instructions to the army

5. The fall of Jericho

V. Questions for discussion:
1. What do you mean when you say, "I'm proud to be a Jew"?
2. Compare the people who left Egypt with those who entered Canaan.
3. What effect would the fall of Jericho have on the Israelites? On the Canaanites?

THINGS TO DO

1. *Spirituals*—Play a phonograph record of the spiritual, "Joshua fought the battle of Jericho." How many other spirituals dealing with Biblical stories do you know? Sing some of these spirituals.

2. *Pageant*—Review the Biblical stories by preparing a pageant called "Great Moments in Jewish History." The following scenes might be included:

a. Abraham, the First Hebrew
b. Isaac and Rebecca
c. The Reunion of Jacob and Esau
d. Joseph and the Brothers in Egypt
e. Moses and the First Passover
f. At Sinai
g. Moses on Mount Nebo

SCRAMBLED NAMES—A PUZZLE

Unscramble the following names. When properly arranged the letters will spell out the names of people or places mentioned in this chapter.

1. Laglig
2. Arabh
3. Androj

4. Aaannc
5. Cheiroj
6. Ajhuos

CHAPTER II

BE STRONG AND OF GOOD
COURAGE!

I. DEFEAT AND VICTORY

THE NEXT CITY which stood in the way of Joshua's advance was Ai.

Again Joshua sent spies saying, "Go up and spy out the land."

The spies returned with a cheerful message. "Send only a small part of the army," they advised, "for Ai is a weak city."

Joshua sent 3000 soldiers against Ai. The men of Ai attacked suddenly, however, and defeated the Israelites.

Joshua and the people were very sad. "When the Canaanites hear of our defeat, they will surround us and destroy us," thought Joshua.

What was wrong? Had they been too sure of victory? Perhaps they had sinned?

Joshua examined the people and soon learned that his commands had been disobeyed. One of the members of the tribe of Judah, a man named Achan, had stolen silver and gold and garments in Jericho and had hidden these precious things in the ground beneath his tent.

After the sinner had been punished Joshua sent another expedition against Ai.

"Be strong and of good courage," said Joshua, "and may God send us victory."

This time Joshua used special strategy. He sent his bravest soldiers at night to lie in wait behind the city.

"Tomorrow I shall attack with the remainder of the army. We shall pretend that we have been beaten again and run away. When the men of Ai pursue after us, rise from your ambush and enter the city."

Joshua's plan worked perfectly. When the men of Ai saw Joshua retreat they boasted, "We have defeated Israel again! Let us pursue after them before they escape!"

As soon as the soldiers of Ai had left the city Joshua raised his javelin. The Israelites rose from their ambush, entered the city and set it on fire.

Joshua and his army now turned around to give battle to the men of Ai who were caught between two armies.

Thus did Joshua win a second glorious victory.

2. GIBEON

When the people of Gibeon heard what had happened to Jericho and to Ai, they feared greatly.

"Let us deal wisely," they said, "or our city too will be destroyed."

The people of Gibeon picked several men to act as messengers. They clothed them with worn garments and with torn shoes. In their sacks they put dry crumbs, and on the donkeys they placed old, patched wine-skins.

The messengers came to Joshua whose camp was at Gilgal, a short distance from Gibeon.

"Peace unto you," said the messengers to Joshua.

"Who are you?" asked Joshua. "What country are you from?"

"We come from a far country," replied the men of Gibeon. "We heard of all the wonders performed by God who took Israel out of Egypt. We have come, therefore, to make a treaty of peace with you."

"How do we know that you are not from a nearby city?" asked Joshua.

"Look at our clothes," replied the men of Gibeon. "When we started on our journey our garments and shoes were new. Now they are old and worn. Our bread was hot. Now we have nothing left but dry crumbs. Even our wine-skins have become torn and patched."

Joshua believed their words and made a treaty of peace with them. The messengers returned to Gibeon with the glad news that Joshua had sworn never to make war against them.

A few days later Joshua's spies came to Gibeon, and learned of the trick played upon them by the men of Gibeon.

Joshua was very angry, but he warned Israel not to harm the city of Gibeon.

"We have sworn unto God," said Joshua, "and we dare not break our oath."

Thus Gibeon was saved from destruction. The men of Gibeon remained in the midst of Israel forever after, and they served as hewers of wood and drawers of water.

3. "SUN, STAND THOU STILL"

When the king of Jerusalem heard that Gibeon had made peace with Israel he became very angry.

He sent word to the kings of four other cities, saying, "Come let us go up against Gibeon and destroy it, for Gibeon has made peace with Joshua."

The king of Jerusalem and his four allies gathered a large army and laid siege to Gibeon.

In great fear, Gibeon sent messengers to Joshua.

"Come quickly!" pleaded the messengers. "You have sworn to aid us in time of trouble. Help, or we shall all be destroyed!"

Joshua promised quick help.

He gathered his soldiers together and said, "Let us take the enemy by surprise! Let us go up quickly against them before they suspect our coming."

Joshua and his soldiers left their camp at Gilgal during the night. Silently they marched until they were behind the king of Jerusalem and his allies. At dawn they attacked.

Taken completely by surprise, the king of Jerusalem and his soldiers fled in terror.

"Quick," cried Joshua, "pursue after them so that they will not be able to form another army against us."

As the enemy fled a strange thing happened. A storm

came up, and hailstones fell upon the fleeing soldiers.

The storm caused great harm to the enemy, but hardly touched the Israelites who were far in the rear.

At first Joshua was overjoyed, for now his army could easily overtake the enemy. The overcast, cloudy skies, however, made it possible for the enemy to hide without being seen.

"If the day were only clear," thought Joshua, "then no enemy soldier could escape!"

Just then the sun came from behind the clouds. All was clear in the strong daylight sun. Before them the Israelites could easily see the escaping soldiers.

Joshua rejoiced at this favorable turn of events and said:

"Sun, stand thou still upon Gibeon;
And thou, moon, in the valley of Aijalon."

Joshua's wish was granted. The sun shone brightly for the remainder of the day. It seemed indeed as if the sun stood still and the day had been lengthened.

"Will night never descend?" thought the fleeing enemy.

One of the Israelite soldiers saw the king of Jerusalem and the four other enemy kings hide in a large cave. Quickly the Israelites rolled large stones to cover up the mouth of the cave so that none could escape.

There was no place to hide! All were captured!

Thus, Joshua won his third great victory, and destroyed the might of the great kings of central and southern Canaan.

EXERCISES

I. Arrange these sentences in the order in which the events occurred in the story. (Review section 1, pages 28 to 29.)

1. Achan was punished for stealing silver and gold and garments.
2. The spies said, "Send only a small part of the army, for Ai is a weak city."
3. Joshua raised his javelin and the men in ambush entered the city and set it on fire.
4. Joshua won a second glorious victory.
5. Joshua was sad because his soldiers were defeated.
6. Joshua sent his bravest soldiers to lie in wait behind the city.
7. Joshua sent spies saying, "Go up and spy out the land."
8. Joshua and his army turned around to give battle to the men of Ai who were caught between two armies.

II. Who said—Joshua or the men of Gibeon? (Review section 2, pages 29 to 31.)

1. "Let us deal wisely or our city too will be destroyed."
2. "Who are you? What country are you from?"
3. "We come from a far country."
4. "How do we know you are not from a nearby city?"
5. "When we started on our journey our garments and shoes were new. Now they are old and worn."
6. "We have sworn unto God, and we dare not break our oath."

III. Complete each sentence. (Review section 3, pages 31 to 32.)

Aijalon, Gibeon, Gilgal, Jerusalem, Joshua

1. Five kings attacked the city of _____.
2. The Israelites were encamped at _____.
3. The enemy was led by the king of _____.
4. _____ made a surprise attack by marching at night.
5. "Sun, stand thou still upon Gibeon; And thou, moon, in the valley of _____."

IV. Questions for discussion:

1. Why is this chapter called, "Be strong and of good courage"? Suggest other titles.
2. "Joshua was a great general". Do you agree or disagree with this statement? Bring proof from the events mentioned in this chapter.
3. Did Joshua do the right thing in protecting Gibeon from attack by the five kings? Why?

THINGS TO DO

1. *Greetings and Farewells*—"*Cha-zak ve-e-matz!*" are the Hebrew words for "Be strong and of good courage!" This phrase is often used in parting from a friend.

Your teacher will help you learn the Hebrew words for other common greetings or expressions of farewell.

Some of the well-known expressions are: "Peace" (Hello or good-bye), "Sabbath Peace," "Happy Holiday", "A Happy New Year", "Welcome", "Good Luck!"

How many of these Hebrew expressions can you memorize?

2. *Class Newspaper*—Prepare a newspaper in which exciting events from the days of Joshua are reported. These are some of the topics that might be assigned to the reporters:

(1) "I saw Jericho"—an eye-witness report by one of the spies

(2) How the walls tumbled down!

(3) An interview with Rahab after the fall of Jericho

(4) An editorial after the defeat at Ai

(5) How we defeated Ai!

(6) A letter from the king of Gibeon to Joshua

(7) Science column—a weather report for the day that the sun stood still

(8) Sports—archery and javelin-throwing contests among the soldiers

(9) A letter from a soldier of the tribe of Reuben to his family east of the Jordan

(10) Drawings: crossing the Jordan; marching around Jericho; the messengers of Gibeon

NUMBER-LETTER PUZZLE

If letters of the alphabet are substituted for the numbers, the words will spell out the slogan which helped Joshua in battle.

2	5					
19	20	18	15	14	7	
1	14	4				
15	ō					
7	15	15	4			
3	15	21	18	1	7	5

CHAPTER III

JOSHUA—FIRST IN PEACE

1. THE DIVISION OF THE LAND

THERE WERE still many battles to be fought. Each city in Canaan had its own king. Most of the cities were protected by walls.

All in all, Joshua fought against the kings of 31 cities. There was war for seven years.

At last there was peace. Many of the Canaanites did not fight against the Israelites, but lived peacefully with them side by side.

The children of Israel had won a strong foothold in the land, especially in the hill-country. Thanks to Joshua's great leadership, the children of Israel now had a land of their own. They had found a home in the promised land.

From now on the land was called *Eretz Yisrael*, the Land of Israel, instead of Canaan. This would always be the land of the Hebrew people. And even in the future when the nation was defeated and exiled, the people would not rest until they had returned to their homeland.

The high priest, Eleazar, the son of Aaron, and the

other *Kohanim* brought the tabernacle and the ark of God to a city named Shiloh.

Joshua called the leaders of the tribes to Shiloh and said, "God has kept His promise to Abraham, Isaac and Jacob. He has given us this land as an inheritance. Now let us cast lots so that each tribe may receive its portion."

Joshua and Eleazar cast lots. Two tribes, Judah and Simeon, won portions in the south. This land was excellent for raising sheep. Dan was given the land to the west where the Philistines still controlled the coast of the Mediterranean Sea.

Joshua's tribe, Ephraim, and half of Manasseh were given the hill-country of central Canaan. On the slopes of the hills the farmers could plant grain and olive-trees and vineyards. The section near Jericho and Ai which Joshua had won in his early battles was assigned to Benjamin.

The four remaining tribes, Asher, Zebulun, Issachar and Naphtali were given portions in the north near the harp-shaped Sea of Kinneret. Here there was excellent farm-land for growing wheat and barley and fruit.

The Levites did not receive a special portion. Instead they were assigned cities in each tribe so that they could serve as priests and as teachers for all Israel.

The 12 tribes were now ready to build their homes and cities in peace.

2. THE RETURN OF THE 2½ TRIBES

Joshua then called the leaders of the tribes of Reuben, Gad and half the tribe of Manasseh.

"You have kept your promise," said Joshua. "You have fought bravely side by side with your brothers until we conquered the land which God promised unto Abraham, Isaac and Jacob. Now you may return to your cities east of the Jordan which Moses gave unto you as an inheritance. Only remember to love the Lord your God and to serve him with all your hearts and with all your souls."

The children of Reuben, of Gad and of the half-tribe of Manasseh departed from Shiloh. They reached the Jordan where they set up a great altar. Then they crossed the Jordan and returned to their homes.

When Israel heard that the 2½ tribes had built an altar, there was great anger.

"What have they done?" asked the children of Israel. "They have built an altar to false gods to lead us astray."

Eleazar's son, Phineas, was picked as a messenger to find out what had happened. With him were ten princes, one for each tribe of Israel west of the Jordan.

They came to the 2½ tribes and said, "Why have you done this evil thing? Did not Moses warn us not to worship false gods?"

Then the children of Reuben and Gad and the half-tribe of Manasseh answered, "God is our witness that we have done nothing wrong. Not to sacrifice to false gods did we build this altar. We were afraid that in the future your children would say that we are not part of Israel because the Jordan separates us from you. Therefore we built this great altar as a sign that the Lord of Israel is

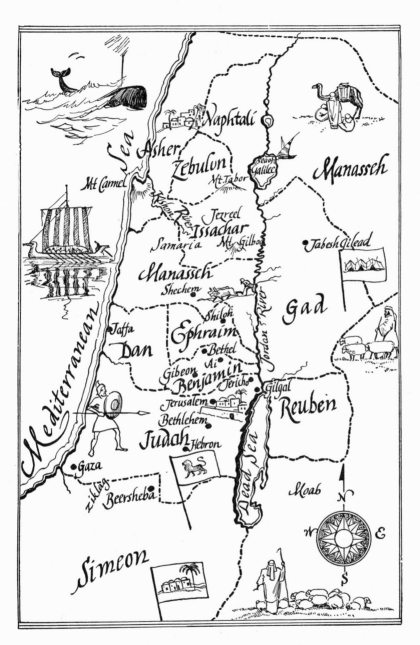

THE TWELVE TRIBES OF ISRAEL

our God. We are one nation and we worship one God."

Phineas and the princes were greatly pleased when they heard these words, and brought back a peaceful report to Joshua.

"Let this be a sign," said Joshua, "that the children of Israel must always be united in serving one God."

3. THE LAST DAYS OF JOSHUA

Joshua had been first in war; now he was first in peace. Joshua dwelt with the other members of the tribe of Ephraim in the central hill-country.

Here Joshua judged the people. The tribes sent their leaders to Joshua for help and for advice.

And Joshua said, "Now that the land has peace, we can fulfill our promise to Joseph. For Joseph made his brothers swear that his bones would be buried in the land of his fathers."

Joseph was then buried in a field near the city of Shechem where Jacob and his twelve sons had once lived.

The children of Israel who had been shepherds in Egypt now had to learn how to farm the land. They learned from their neighbors how to plant barley and wheat. They also grew many fruits such as figs, dates, pomegranates, olives and grapes.

From the fruits of the trees they made honey, and from the flocks they obtained milk. Their land was indeed a land flowing with milk and with honey.

In the spring and summer the sun shone brightly. No clouds darkened the skies. But in the winter strong rains came down from heaven to water the fields.

"Where shall we find water to drink in summer?" asked the children of Israel. The lack of wells and rivers had been the curse of all who settled in the hill-country.

Soon, however, the children of Israel learned to dig deep holes called cisterns. These cisterns they lined with waterproof lime plaster. The rains came down in the winter, and the waters were stored in the cisterns. Thus there was so much water, even in the dry season, that the children of Israel could sing, "My cup runneth over."

Recently, many of these villages have been dug up. From the ruins of these villages we have discovered the great secret which helped the children of Israel to live in prosperity. By learning how to line the cisterns with waterproof plaster the Israelites had won the battle against lack of water. And water in the East means life!

Joshua served as leader for about 28 years. Knowing that death was approaching, Joshua called the people together to Shechem for his final message.

There were tears in the eyes of the people as they glanced at their leader. It was Joshua who had led them to victory against the Amalekites in the desert. It was Joshua who had served Moses when the ten commandments were granted at Sinai. It was Joshua who had brought them into the promised land, and who had wisely divided the land among the 12 tribes.

And Joshua said, "Our father Abraham came to Canaan from beyond the river. And Abraham served God. And God made a covenant with Abraham that this land would be given unto his children. And when the children of Israel became slaves in Egypt, God sent Moses to free them from slavery. And God gave us the Torah to teach us truth and justice. And God brought us back to this land as He had promised.

"Now tell me this day whom you will choose. If you will serve God, then God will bless you. But if you follow strange gods then you will surely be punished."

And the people answered, "We will serve God with all our hearts and with all our souls!"

Joshua then blessed the people who departed unto their homes. Joshua died at a ripe old age, and the children of Israel mourned for their great leader who had brought them into the promised land.

EXERCISES

I. Choose the correct word or name. (Review section 1, pages 36 to 37.)

1. Joshua fought against _____ kings. (3, 31)
2. Israel conquered much land in the _____. (hill-country, valleys)
3. The ark was brought to _____. (Jerusalem, Shiloh)
4. Judah was given land in the _____. (north, south)
5. The land given to Ephraim was good for _____. (farming, sheep-raising)

II. True or false? (Review section 2, pages 38 to 40.)

1. The 2½ tribes fought bravely for Israel.
2. The 2½ tribes received land west of the Jordan.
3. The 2½ tribes built an altar near the Jordan River.
4. Phineas and the messengers worshiped at the altar.

5. The 2½ tribes said, "We built this altar as a sign that the Lord of Israel is our God. We are one nation and we worship one God."

III. Answer each question in a complete sentence. (Review section 3, pages 40 to 42.)
1. Where did Joshua live?
2. How did Joshua fulfill the promise made to Joseph by the children of Israel?
3. Why did the villages in the hill-country suffer from lack of water?
4. How did the Israelites store water for the dry season?
5. What promise did the children of Israel make to Joshua before his death?

IV. Questions for discussion:
1. Compare the children of Israel in Joshua's day and the modern *chalutzim*.
2. Why is Joshua considered one of the greatest leaders we have ever had?

THINGS TO DO

1. *Map*—Draw a colored map showing the division of the land among the 12 tribes. Use the colors found in the flags of the 12 tribes:

Tribes east of the Jordan:
Reuben—red
Gad—red and black
Manasseh—black
Southern tribes:
Simeon—green
Judah—azure blue

West:
Dan—sapphire blue (deep blue)
Central:
Benjamin—mixed colors
Ephraim—black
Northern:
Issachar—black
Zebulun—white
Asher—red
Naphtali—wine-red
(Consult page 39 for the boundaries and tribal symbols.)
2. Construct a model of a walled city.

COOPERATIVE STORIES

This game can be lots of fun.

The children of Israel have captured a suspicious-looking person near their camp at Gilgal. They ask him many questions. Each pupil answers the questions on a piece of paper. When the first question has been answered fold over that part of the paper on which you have written and pass to your neighbor. On the paper you have received from your neighbor answer the second question. Fold and pass. Do this until all the questions have been answered. Read the answers. The mixed-up stories should make interesting reading.

Here are some questions that the leader might ask the prisoner:

1. What is your name?
2. Where are you from?
3. Where are you going?
4. Why?
5. What did the children of Israel do to the prisoner?

UNIT TWO

The Judges

CHAPTER IV

DEBORAH—THE WOMAN WHO FREED ISRAEL

1. AT SHILOH

ELEAZAR, the *Kohen Gadol*, and his son Phineas ruled Israel after the death of Joshua.

They were in charge of the tabernacle in Shiloh and of the ark of God. On Sabbaths and festivals the children of Israel came to Shiloh to sacrifice and to pray to God.

On Passover, especially, the children of Israel would crowd into Shiloh. Each year they would hear the glorious tale of how Moses freed Israel from slavery. Since this was the time of the barley harvest, the farmers would bring sheaves of barley unto the house of God as an offering.

On Shavuot the children of Israel would come to celebrate the granting of the ten commandments. The farmers brought grains of wheat and first fruits as an offering.

As the farmer gave the basket to the *Kohen*, or priest, he would say: "God has brought us unto this place, and has given us this land, a land flowing with milk and with

47

honey. And now, behold, I have brought the first of the fruit of the land, which Thou, O Lord, hast given me."

At the turn of the year, on Rosh Ha-Shanah, the children of Israel would celebrate the coming of a new year.

At the time of the grape harvest, or Sukkot, they would build booths or huts as a reminder of the huts in which the Israelites lived as they wandered in the desert.

The maidens of Israel would dance at Shiloh on these festivals, and the people rejoiced in their new land.

Eleazar knew that there would be many problems in the days ahead.

1. Would the 12 tribes remain united?

2. Would the children of Israel continue to worship God, or would they imitate their Canaanite neighbors who worshiped idols?

3. Would the tribes be strong enough to defend themselves against their enemies?

2. A WOMAN JUDGE

When Eleazar and Phineas died, the people forgot the commands of Joshua. There was no leader to unite the 12 tribes. The farmers watched their neighbors worship false gods, and began to do the same. The Canaanites made war against the tribes, and there was none to defend Israel.

From time to time a leader would arise to unite the people and to remind them of the teachings of Moses and Joshua. These leaders were called Judges.

One of the greatest of these Judges was a woman named

Deborah. She lived with the tribe of Ephraim not far from Shiloh.

There she sat under a palm-tree and judged wisely all who came to her.

"Hear my case," pleaded a shepherd. "The people of my village deny me the right to pasture my sheep in the woods, since my family belongs to another tribe."

"The woods are free for all to pasture their sheep," ruled Deborah.

The elders of the village heard and obeyed.

"I am a widow, and I have no bread to eat," wept a woman before Deborah.

"Follow the gleaners in the fields. The grain that drops from their hands to the ground you may pick up, and keep. Thus did Moses teach us."

The people loved and honored the wise judge.

At that time the Canaanites under Captain Sisera began to treat the Israelites with cruelty. Sisera had 900 chariots of iron, and the people feared him.

His soldiers would come to Israel at harvest time.

"Your wheat and your fruits belong to us," they shouted.

The soldiers would return later and steal ploughs and tools. They would use the bronze and iron to fashion swords.

The children of Israel were afraid to travel on the main roads, for Sisera's soldiers would attack them and rob them.

The people came in tears before Deborah.

"Help us! Help us!" they begged.

"I am not a soldier," replied Deborah. "I am but a mother in Israel."

"We will follow you into battle," said the people. "Lead us and we will obey."

"When the proper time comes, then we will fight for our freedom," answered Deborah.

Deborah searched for a brave soldier to lead Israel into battle. Her messengers brought word of many brave men who resisted when the Canaanites attacked.

"There is one man in the north who has openly defied the Canaanites," the messengers told Deborah. "His name is Barak."

After Deborah had heard many reports of Barak's bravery she said, "Barak is the man who must lead Israel into battle. Barak means 'lightning'. Perhaps he will strike like lightning, and Israel will be free once more."

3. THE DEFEAT OF SISERA

Deborah sent word to Barak: "You must lead Israel against Sisera. May God grant you victory!"

Barak replied, "If you go with me, then I will go. But I will not go without you!"

"Gladly will I go," answered Deborah, "but it will not be to your honor for people to say that a woman led Israel to victory."

Deborah met Barak at Mount Tabor in the north. They sent messengers to all the tribes of Israel asking for help. Israel was so disunited that many of the tribes ignored the messengers.

Those tribes who had been most oppressed by Sisera, such as Zebulun, Issachar, Manasseh and Benjamin, answered the call. Deborah's tribe of Ephraim and Barak's tribe of Naphtali sent large numbers of men.

In all, Barak had 10,000 soldiers at his command.

Sisera mocked when he heard of Barak's rebellion. "Our chariots and horsemen will destroy those farmers. They do not have even swords and spears."

"We shall be rich with spoil," laughed Sisera's mother. "Bring back all the dyed and embroidered garments you can find in the Israelite villages," she added.

"And lots of slaves," said Sisera.

The proud Canaanite captain led his 900 chariots and his soldiers toward the brook Kishon.

"Up!" said Deborah to Barak. "This is the day on which the Lord has delivered the enemy into your hands."

Deborah and Barak marched to meet the Canaanites. Could they defeat such a strong enemy?

Just then a great storm broke out. The roads turned to mud. Sisera's chariots were embedded in the mud, and could not move forward. The horses fell on the slippery roads.

The few chariots that escaped from the muddy roads began to advance across the brook Kishon.

But the tiny brook had been changed by the storm into a swirling river. The mad flood-waters hurled horse and rider into the river, and swept them to their death.

"Victory is ours!" shouted Deborah and Barak.

Quickly they advanced on foot and attacked the frightened Canaanites.

Seeing that his army had been defeated, Sisera alighted from his chariot and fled. He sought refuge in the tent of Jael, a Kenite woman whose sheep were grazing not far from the battle-front.

Jael gave Sisera food and a place to sleep. Although Jael was not an Israelite she knew how much the Israelites had suffered at the hands of Sisera. She quietly slew him as he slept, thus putting an end to his proud boasts.

Deborah then sang a joyous song of rejoicing:

"I, unto the Lord will I sing;
I will sing praise to the Lord, the God of Israel.
The stars in their courses fought against Sisera.
The brook Kishon swept them away!"

Deborah continued to rule Israel in peace for many years. Deborah might well be called the Joan of Arc of the Bible. She was the only woman in days of old to win freedom for Israel by leading the soldiers into battle.

The land had peace for forty years.

EXERCISES

I. Match. (Review section 1, pages 47 to 48.)

Column A	Column B
Eleazar	1. Grape harvest
Passover	2. First fruits
Shavuot	3. Barley harvest
Shiloh	4. *Kohen Gadol*
Sukkot	5. City where the ark rested

THE DEFEAT OF SISERA

II. Who said to whom? (Review section 2, pages 48 to 50.)

   1. "The people of my village deny me the right to pasture my sheep in the woods."

   2. "The woods are free for all to pasture their sheep."

   3. "Your wheat and your fruits belong to us."

   4. "I am but a mother in Israel."

   5. "We will follow you into battle."

III. What is my name? (Review section 3, pages 50 to 52.)

   1. I was a woman judge who led the troops to victory.

   2. I was a soldier from the tribe of Naphtali who fought against the Canaanites. The people called me "Lightning."

   3. I am a mountain on which 10,000 Israelites gathered to fight for freedom.

   4. I was a proud captain who commanded 900 chariots.

   5. I am a brook, but the Canaanites drowned in my flood-waters.

   6. I was a woman in whose tent the captain of the Canaanites sought refuge.

IV. Questions for discussion:

   1. Which problems faced the children of Israel in the days of the Judges? How did they solve these problems?

   2. The children of Israel found new reasons for celebrating the holidays when they became farmers. What were the new reasons?

THINGS TO DO

1. *Research*—Find out about some other great Jewish woman of today or of the past.

2. *Dance*—Learn an Israeli dance showing how the farmer works the soil, or a dance appropriate for one of the holidays.

GUESS MY TRIBE

In this game, two students select the name of one of the 12 tribes. The other students try to guess the name of the tribe. The first one to guess the correct name picks a partner. The two new partners select another tribal name.

(Consult pages 43-44 for the names of the 12 tribes.)

CHAPTER V

GIDEON—THE JUDGE
WHO WOULD NOT BE KING

1. A NEW HERO

AFTER THE DEATH of Deborah, the children of Israel forgot God.

Their sons married Canaanite girls, and their daughters married Canaanite men. When harvest time came the Canaanites bowed down to an idol named Baal.

"Baal has blessed our flocks and our fields," they said.

The children of Israel, too, set up images of Baal, and worshiped the idol.

From the east came swarms of Midianite and Amalekite soldiers. They covered the land like locusts and stole the grain and the fruits that the children of Israel had planted.

Those who resisted were tortured or put to death. In terror the children of Israel fled and hid in caves or in the mountains.

One brave man who did not lose courage was Gideon of the tribe of Manasseh. At harvest time Gideon did not run away. He hid his grain in the wine-press and there threshed the grain.

On Passover, Gideon would pray, "O Lord, God, who took us out of slavery in Egypt, deliver us once again from bondage."

Once as Gideon prayed he heard the voice of God. "I have picked you to save Israel. But first destroy the altar to Baal."

That night Gideon and ten faithful men broke the image and the altar of Baal.

The next morning the Hebrew villagers awoke and heard what Gideon had done. They came to his house and said to Gideon's father, "Your son shall surely die for he has destroyed the image and the altar of Baal."

Then Gideon's father replied, "Do you fight for Baal? If he is a god let him fight for himself and punish my son!"

The villagers were ashamed and went away.

Many Israelites now began to follow the brave Gideon. When the Midianites and Amalekites again invaded the land, Gideon blew the *shofar* and proclaimed, "All who are for the Lord follow me!"

Thousands of Israelites swarmed to Gideon's camp in the valley of Jezreel ready to do battle.

2. FOR THE LORD AND FOR GIDEON!

That night God appeared unto Gideon and said, "I shall bring victory by means of a few men. Let the others return to their tents,"

Gideon then addressed his soldiers and said, "God does not need a large army for victory. All who wish, may return to their tents."

Many of the Israelites returned but thousands still remained. Gideon then ordered his soldiers to drink from the waters of Ein-harod.

It was at the heat of the day, at noontime, and the soldiers were hot and thirsty. Most of the soldiers bent down on their knees to drink. Others cupped the water in their hands, and lapped the water with their tongues.

Gideon chose the 300 men who had lapped the water. Those who had bent down were sent away.

Why were those who bent down sent away? Perhaps Gideon suspected them of having bent down before, in worship to idols. At any rate, Gideon felt that 300 men were enough for the surprise raid he planned against the enemy.

That night Gideon said to his servant, "Come, let us spy on the Midianite camp."

Before them stretched the huge Midianite army. In the camp were thousands of camels on which the Midianites placed all the silver and grain and fruits and booty which they could rob.

Gideon and his servant climbed on a rock behind the Midianite camp and secretly listened to the conversation of two soldiers.

"Listen to a strange dream," said one soldier to his friend. "I dreamed that a cake of barley bread tumbled into the camp of Midian. It came up to one tent and fell upon it, turning it over so that the tent lay flat. Isn't this a strange dream?"

"It is a frightening dream," replied his friend, "for it means that the sword of Gideon, captain of Israel, will destroy us all."

Gideon was overjoyed when he heard the interpretation of the dream.

Quickly returning to his camp, Gideon said to his 300 men, "Arise, for the Lord has delivered into your hands the army of Midian!"

Gideon divided the 300 men into three companies of a hundred each. Each soldier was given a torch, a horn and a pitcher.

"Follow me to the camp of Midian," he said. "When I give the signal break the pitchers with a loud noise. Blow the horns and shout. Then by the light of the torches attack the enemy."

The men followed Gideon to the camp of Midian. At the given signal they broke their pitchers against the rocks, making a great noise.

They blew the horn and shouted, "For the Lord and for Gideon! For the Lord and for Gideon!"

The Midianites awoke in the middle of the night at the terrible sound of the shouting. Never before had they fought at night. All around them they saw lighted torches and heard the shout, "For the Lord and for Gideon!"

"We are lost!" cried the Midianites. In great terror the Midianite soldiers began to strike in the dark. The Israelites had not yet attacked, but the Midianites imagined that a great army had already invaded their tents. Blindly the Midianites struck at each other, wounding and killing their own soldiers.

"Flee for your lives," they shouted.

Before dawn the battle was over and Gideon with but 300 men had won a great victory.

Thankful to their brave hero, the children of Israel came to Gideon and said, "Rule over us. Be our king. After you, your son will rule and your son's son, for you have delivered us from our enemy."

And Gideon replied, "I shall not be your king, for only God is your ruler."

Gideon judged Israel for 40 years, and there was peace in the land.

3. THE SON WHO WANTED TO BE KING

Gideon refused to be king. His son Abimelech was different. In the heart of his son there was a burning desire to be king.

Gideon had many sons. They were kind and good like their father. But Abimelech was wicked and evil.

"When my father dies," said Abimelech, "I shall become king over Israel."

"What will your brothers say?" asked his friends. "You are not the oldest of Gideon's sons."

"I shall know how to take care of my brothers," replied Abimelech.

Gideon had several wives as was the custom for rulers in those days. The mother of Abimelech was not Gideon's favorite wife. Abimelech hated his half-brothers, and planned their death.

As soon as Gideon had died, Abimelech hired wicked men to slay his brothers. Only the youngest son, Jotham, escaped.

Abimelech then went to Shechem where his mother's family lived. The men whom he had hired shouted, "Long live King Abimelech! Long live King Abimelech!"

The people of Shechem joined in the shouting, for they said, "He is from our own city." Thus Abimelech became king of Shechem.

Jotham, the youngest son of Gideon, escaped to the top of Mount Gerizim, which overlooks Shechem.

Standing on top of the mount, Jotham shouted, "Men of Shechem, hear my words."

The mountain is so formed that the voice carries clearly to the city at the foot of the mount. The people listened as Jotham told this story:

The trees once decided to select a king. They said to the olive-tree, "Reign over us."

But the olive-tree refused, saying, "Shall I leave my fruits and my rich, fat oil to be king?"

The trees said to the fig-tree, "Come, reign over us."

"What?" answered the fig-tree. "Shall I leave my sweetness and my good fruit to reign over you?"

The trees then turned to the vine, "Be our king."

The vine too refused saying, "Should I leave my grapes, and my wine which gladdens the heart of man, to be king of the trees?"

At last the trees came to the thorn, and said, "We want you as our king."

Said the thorn tree, "If in truth you make me your king, then come and find protection in my shadow. But if not, then let a fire come from the thorn and devour the trees of Lebanon."

"You have made Abimelech your king when better men than he refused to be king," continued Jotham. "If you are sincere and will serve him willingly, then may he be your protector. But if you are not sincere, then let a fire come from Abimelech and destroy Shechem, and let a fire come from Shechem and destroy Abimelech."

Jotham then fled to another city.

The men of Shechem were sad when they heard Jotham's story. They knew that he spoke truly. Instead of picking a good king, they had picked a wicked king. But it was too late!

For three years Abimelech served as king of Shechem. He was very cruel to his subjects. After three years the people rebelled. Abimelech put down the rebellion with great cruelty.

Abimelech and his soldiers now laid siege to one of the nearby cities. Abimelech seized the bough of a tree and tried to set fire to the tower of the city.

A woman in the besieged city cast a stone from the tower as Abimelech approached. The stone broke his skull.

"Kill me with your sword!" pleaded Abimelech with his armor-bearer. "Let not people say that Abimelech was slain by a woman."

The armor-bearer thrust him through with the sword, thus ending his wicked career.

The people were pleased that Abimelech could no longer harm them. They had learned that only a good leader deserves to rule.

EXERCISES

I. Why? (Review section 1, pages 56 to 57.)
   1. Why did the children of Israel hide in the caves?
   2. Why did Gideon thresh the grain in the wine-press?
   3. Why did the villagers want to kill Gideon?
   4. Why did the villagers allow Gideon to go unharmed?
   5. Why did the children of Israel gather in the valley of Jezreel?

II. True or false? (Review section 2, pages 57 to 60.)
   1. Gideon wanted a large army.
   2. Gideon picked as soldiers those who bent down.
   3. The dream cheered Gideon because he now felt certain of victory.
   4. The Midianites were surprised by a night attack.
   5. Gideon wanted to be king.

III. Choose the correct name—Abimelech or Jotham. (Review section 3, pages 60 to 63.)
   1. _____ was Gideon's youngest son.
   2. _____ slew Gideon's sons.
   3. _____ told the story of how the thorn became king of the trees.
   4. _____ served as king after Gideon's death.
   5. After 3 years the people of Shechem rebelled against

IV. Questions for discussion:

   1. What good qualities does a leader need? Which Hebrew leaders had these qualities?

   2. In which ways did Gideon resemble the olive, fig
and vine? In which ways did Abimelech resemble
the thorn?

THINGS TO DO

1, *Original Story*—The Bible does not tell us what happened to Jotham after he fled from Abimelech. Write a story
telling what became of Jotham. Let the ending be a happy
one.

2. *Dramatization*—Dramatize the story of Gideon. Divide
the play into the following scenes:

Scene 1—Gideon destroys the altar of Baal; Scene 2—
Gideon chooses his army; Scene 3—Gideon attacks Midian;
Scene 4—Gideon refuses the kingship; Scene 5—Abimelech
and Jotham.

A PUZZLE

Answer these questions. The initial letters of the answers
will spell out the name of a well-known tribe.

   1. What enemy nation did Gideon defeat?

   2. Who reigned as king after the death of Gideon?

   3. To which tribe did Barak belong?

   4. Who was the first Hebrew?

   5. At what mountain were the 10 commandments proclaimed?

   6. Which captain of the Canaanites was defeated by
Deborah?

   7. To which tribe did Joshua belong?

   8. Near which city were Abraham, Isaac and Jacob buried?

CHAPTER VI

THE STORY OF RUTH

I. THE FAITHFUL RUTH

AND IT CAME to pass, in the days when the Judges judged, that there was a famine in the land. The early rain did not fall in the winter, nor did the late rain fall in the springtime.

The wells ran dry; the barley and the wheat shriveled up. And the people cried for bread and for water.

Elimelech, a farmer who lived in Bethlehem, said to his wife, "I have heard that there is food in the land of Moab. Let us go to Moab so that we will live and not die."

Elimelech and his wife, Naomi, took their two sons, and traveled from Bethlehem, which is in the tribe of Judah, to the land of Moab.

When they arrived in Moab, the father became ill and died.

The two sons grew up in Moab and were married there. Mahlon, the older brother, married a girl named Ruth, and Chilion, the younger brother, married a girl named Orpah.

But a plague broke out in Moab and the two sons died in the plague. Naomi was now a widow and childless.

Naomi had been in Moab for about ten years. The famine had long since ended in Bethlehem, and Naomi decided to return to her own city.

And Naomi said to her two daughters-in-law, "Return to the home of your parents. May God deal kindly with you, as you have dealt with my sons and with me."

Both Ruth and Orpah wept and replied, "We shall stay with you."

But Naomi answered, "Please turn back, my daughters."

Orpah kissed Naomi, said farewell, and returned to her own family. Ruth, however, would not leave Naomi for she loved her and knew that Naomi needed her help.

And Naomi said to Ruth, "Behold, your sister-in-law has gone back unto her family. Return after your sister-in-law."

But Ruth replied," Entreat me not to leave you, and to return from following after you. For whither you go, I will go; and where you lodge, I will lodge. Your people will be my people; and your God, my God. Naught but death will part you and me."

Naomi kissed her faithful daughter-in-law, and both set out together on the road to Bethlehem.

2. IN THE FIELD OF BOAZ

When Naomi arrived in Bethlehem, her neighbors were surprised to see how much she had aged and how sad she looked.

They said, "Is this Naomi? Is this the person of whom we used to say that Naomi (pleasantness) is a name that is very fitting for such a beautiful woman?"

Naomi and Ruth had arrived in Bethlehem at the time of the barley harvest. And Ruth said to Naomi, "Let me now go to the field and glean after the reapers among the sheaves of grain."

And Naomi said, "Go, my daughter."

It was the rule in ancient Israel that the reaper could not pick up the grain that fell to the ground. This grain belonged to the widow, the orphan and the poor who gleaned after the reaper. Thus, no one need go hungry.

Ruth happened to enter the field of Boaz, a wealthy farmer who was related to Elimelech. Ruth turned to the maiden reapers and said, "Let me glean, I pray you, and gather after the reapers among the sheaves."

The maidens consented, and Ruth gleaned in the field for several hours.

Boaz came into the field before noon.

"May God be with you," he said to the reapers.

"May He bless you," they answered.

Seeing Ruth in the field, Boaz asked his servant, "Who is this young woman?"

"This is Ruth, the daughter-in-law of Naomi. She came with Naomi from the land of Moab," replied the servant.

Boaz turned to Ruth and said, "Do not glean in any other field. I have ordered all the workers to treat you kindly. When you are thirsty, go to the vessels and drink of the water which my young men have drawn."

"You are very thoughtful," said Ruth.

"I have heard how kind you have been to your mother-in-law, Naomi," replied Boaz. "May God reward you for your kindness."

At meal-time Boaz called to Ruth saying, "Please come here and partake of our bread and food."

Ruth joined Boaz and the reapers and partook of their food.

After their meal Boaz whispered to the reapers, "Purposely let some of the sheaves drop to the ground. Make certain that she gathers enough grain to last her for several days."

Then Boaz said to Ruth, "Do not go tomorrow to any other field. Remain with us until the end of the harvest."

Naomi was amazed to see the large amount of barley which Ruth had gathered.

"Where did you glean?" she asked.

"In the field of Boaz," answered Ruth. "He was very kind to me."

"He is related to us," said Naomi. "He is a very kind-hearted man."

"He has invited me to glean in his field until the end of the harvest," added Ruth.

"I am grateful for his kindness," said Naomi. "It is a good thing indeed for you to glean with his maidens, for then no harm will come to you."

And Ruth gleaned in the field of Boaz until the end of the barley harvest and of the wheat harvest.

RUTH IN THE FIELDS OF BETHLEHEM

3. RUTH'S REWARD

At the end of the harvest season, Naomi said to Ruth, "The harvest is over. We must find out whether Boaz, who is a close relative, will redeem you or not."

"What do you advise that I do?" asked Ruth.

"He is in his threshing-floor tonight," answered Naomi, "threshing out the wheat. Go to him tonight and ask whether he will perform his duty as kinsman."

It was the custom in ancient Israel for the nearest kinsman to marry a childless widow. The children of such a marriage would keep alive the name of the one who had died.

Ruth went to Boaz as Naomi had advised.

"Gladly would I carry out the duty of the kinsman," said Boaz. "But there is a closer relative. We must seek his permission first."

When Naomi heard from Ruth what had happened she said, "Now all will be well. Boaz will not rest until he has finished this matter."

The next day Boaz went to the gate of the city. As he sat there, he saw his relative passing by.

"Come here," said Boaz to the kinsman. "There is an important matter for us to discuss."

The kinsman sat down near Boaz by the gate of the city. Boaz then gathered ten elders of the city to serve as witnesses.

"Naomi," said Boaz, "is selling a parcel of land that belonged to Elimelech. Since you are the closest relative it is your duty to redeem the land. Will you buy the land? If you do not redeem the land, then I, as the next closest relative, shall redeem it."

The kinsman replied, "I shall redeem it."

Then added Boaz, "On the day that you buy the land, you must also redeem Ruth so that the name of Mahlon will not be forgotten."

"This I cannot do lest I spoil my own inheritance," answered the kinsman. "I transfer my rights to you."

In ancient days as a sign of a business transaction the seller would remove his sandal and give it to the buyer. This was a sign of a transfer of rights.

The kinsman withdrew his sandal handing it to Boaz who said, "The elders are witness that I have redeemed this land with the money that I shall give to Naomi. Also, I shall carry out my duty to Ruth and marry her so that the name of Mahlon will not be forgotten."

Ruth was very happy to be the wife of the kind Boaz, and Boaz loved the beautiful and faithful Ruth.

A child was born to Boaz and to Ruth whom they named Obed.

And Naomi rejoiced saying, "This shall be to me as my own grandchild, for his mother has been dearer to me than seven sons."

When Obed grew up he became the father of Jesse who was the father of David. And David was the greatest king that Israel ever had.

Ruth's loyalty had been rewarded. Even though she was of foreign birth, because of her good character she was picked by God to be the great-grandmother of Israel's noblest king.

The beautiful story of Ruth and Naomi will never be forgotten. Each year on Shavuot, the holiday of the harvest and of the first fruits, we read this story which took place at harvest-time in the days of the Judges.

EXERCISES

I. Complete. (Review section 1, pages 65 to 66.)

Bethlehem, Mahlon, Moab, Naomi, Orpah, Ruth

1. Elimelech lived in the city of _____.
2. The wife of Elimelech was named _____.
3. Elimelech's older son was named _____.
4. Because of the famine Elimelech went to live in the land of _____.
5. After the death of her husband, Naomi's daughter-in-law _____ returned to her own family.
6. _____ said, "Entreat me not to leave you."

II. Who said to whom? (Review section 2, pages 66 to 68.)

1. "Let me now go to the field and glean after the reapers among the sheaves of grain."
2. "Who is this young woman?"
3. "This is Ruth, the daughter-in-law of Naomi. She came with Naomi from the land of Moab."
4. "Do not glean in any other field."
5. "Make certain that she gathers enough grain to last her for several days."
6. "It is a good thing indeed for you to glean with his maidens, for then no harm will come to you."

III. What is my name? (Review section 3, pages 70 to 72.)

1. I lost my husband and my two sons. Ruth was as dear to me as my own child.
2. I was born in Moab. God rewarded me for being faithful to Naomi.
3. I married Ruth. I was the older son of Elimelech.
4. I was a wealthy farmer in Bethlehem. I did my duty as a kinsman.
5. I was king in Israel. Ruth was my great-grandmother.

IV. Questions for discussion:

1. Ruth was rewarded by God because of her good character. What good qualities did Ruth show?
2. What are some interesting customs of ancient Israel mentioned in this story?

THINGS TO DO

1. *Memory Gem*—Memorize the words of Ruth to Naomi on page 66, beginning, "Entreat me not to leave you."

2. *Hebrew Names*—Naomi means "pleasantness". Ruth means "friendship." What is your Hebrew name? Were you named after some hero of the Hebrew people?

Make a list of the children in your class. Next to each English name write the Hebrew name.

3. *Shavuot Songs*—The story of Ruth is read on the holiday of Shavuot. Learn a Shavuot song that tells of the harvest or first fruits. Here are the names of some of these songs:

a. *Bikkurim*
b. *Sa-ley-nu*
c. *Shavuot Chag Nechmad*
d. *Omer, Omer*

FINISH THE JINGLE

Devotion and kindness, goodness and truth
Were the qualities shown by the beautiful _____.

"I will share", said Ruth, "all that which is thine.
Your God is my God, and your nation _____."

In the field of Boaz, dear Ruth could be seen;
She followed the reapers, the barley to _____.

There was bread for Naomi and food to eat
Because Ruth had gleaned the barley and _____.

The praises of Ruth we are happy to sing;
From her was descended a glorious _____.

CHAPTER VII

SAMSON AND THE
PHILISTINES

1. MIGHTY SAMSON

ISRAEL now had to face its greatest enemy. The Philistines, a strong warlike race, had captured all of the cities along the coast.

The Philistines invaded the strongholds of the 12 tribes of Israel. They laid a heavy tax on the children of Israel; they took their tools, their silver and gold, and treated them with great cruelty.

The children of Israel prayed unto God to send a leader to save them from their enemy.

The hero who saved Israel from the Philistines was Samson of the tribe of Dan. When Samson was born his mother said, "I shall raise him as one who is holy unto God."

The mother vowed that Samson would obey the laws of the Nazarites. He would touch no wine or strong drink, nor would his hair be cut. These were the rules of the Nazarites, a group of holy men who devoted their lives to God.

Samson the young Nazarite grew stronger and stronger each day. Even as a boy he could perform great feats of strength. Later, as a young man, when he worked in the fields he could do the work of ten men.

Samson knew that his strength lay in his hair. As long as he kept his vows as a Nazarite he would be strong.

One day as Samson walked along the road a huge beast sprang at him from the bushes. It was a lion.

Samson caught the lion at the throat. A fierce battle ensued. With his bare hands, Samson killed the lion as if it were but a harmless sheep.

The dead lion lay in the road, and all who passed by wondered at the mighty strength of the young Samson.

Samson once visited a Philistine city named Timnah in order to purchase some goods for his family. There he met a young Philistine girl with whom he fell deeply in love.

Upon his return to his home Samson said to his mother and father, "I met a young Philistine girl in Timnah with whom I have fallen in love. Go to her parents and arrange a marriage for I cannot live without her."

"Is there no Israelite girl whom you can marry?" asked his parents. "Why do you choose a Philistine?"

"I love her deeply," replied Samson, "and nothing must stand in the way."

The parents sadly consented and arranged the marriage. A wedding-feast was prepared, but soon there was trouble.

Some of the Philistines at the wedding-feast made sport of Samson and tried to cheat him.

In the quarrel that followed, Samson killed 30 Philistines single-handed.

Samson went back to his father's house, promising to return to Timnah. There was so much to be done, however, on his father's farm that many months passed before Samson visited Timnah.

His father-in-law growing very angry at Samson's absence said, "It is better for my daughter to be married to a Philistine than to an Israelite."

Samson's wife was then given in marriage by her father to a Philistine young man.

Samson was furious when he heard what had happened.

"Now I shall avenge myself on the enemies of my people," shouted Samson.

Samson went to the woods and caught some of the foxes that ran wild in the forests. He tied the tails of the foxes together, and put a torch between each two foxes.

The foxes ran madly through the fields of the Philistines. Soon the grain in the fields caught fire and burnt to the ground.

"Samson's father-in-law is at fault," said the Philistines. "He should not have given Samson's wife in marriage to another. Because of him our fields have been burnt!"

The Philistines came to Timnah and in punishment burnt the girl and her father to death.

Samson angrily shouted, "Those who are guilty of this cruel punishment will pay with their lives."

Samson attacked those who had taken part in this crime, and defeated them single-handed.

When Israel heard of the exploits of Samson, they rejoiced.

"At last we have found a leader," they said, "who can deliver us from the hands of the cruel Philistines."

2. SAMSON THE INVINCIBLE

The Philistines gathered an army to capture mighty Samson.

"Who knows what Samson will do next?" they said anxiously. "Soon all Israel may rebel."

Samson found refuge in the mountains of Judah.

The Philistine army invaded Judah in search for Samson.

"Why have you come up against us?" asked the men of Judah in fear. "We have paid our yearly tribute."

"We have come to bind Samson," answered the Philistines. "We will do to him what he has done to us."

3000 men of Judah went to Samson and said, "What have you done? Don't you know that the Philistines are rulers over us? Don't you know they can destroy us all?"

"As they did unto me, so have I done unto them," replied Samson.

"We have come to bind you," said the men of Judah, "to deliver you into the hands of the Philistines."

And Samson said, "Swear that you will not harm me if I allow you to bind me."

"We will not touch you," they swore.

Samson allowed the men of Judah to bind him with two new ropes, and to take him to the Philistines.

When the Philistines saw Samson bound they shouted, "Samson is our prisoner! Samson is our prisoner!"

At that moment Samson stretched his mighty arms. The ropes became like flax that is burnt with fire. The bands dropped from his arms.

Samson was free!

Looking around for a weapon Samson saw the large jawbone of a donkey lying on the ground.

Seizing the jawbone Samson struck the oncoming Philistines. He struck to the left and to the right. Each blow was a death-blow.

More and more Philistines crowded around the mighty Samson. The jawbone did its deadly work.

At last the Philistines ran in fear with Samson pursuing after them. One man chased an army!

A thousand Philistines died that day.

Samson's next adventure was in Gaza. Samson again fell in love with a Philistine girl. Risking his life Samson went to the city of Gaza to visit the girl.

When night fell the Philistines closed the gate of the city.

"Now Samson cannot escape," said the Philistines.

Samson went to the gate of the city. Seeing the gate was closed, Samson put his hands around the posts which upheld the gate. With one mighty wrench he plucked up the posts, bar and all.

The Philistines were amazed to see Samson march off carrying the giant doors of the city-gate on his shoulders.

He had escaped again.

3. SAMSON AND DELILAH

Samson became the new judge of Israel. The Philistines were afraid to send soldiers to the Israelite cities, for Samson and his men would attack and destroy the Philistines.

The Israelites stopped paying tribute and were free once more.

Samson ruled for twenty years.

At last his love for Philistine women proved to be his downfall. Samson now fell in love with a Philistine woman named Delilah.

The Philistine lords came to Delilah and promised her a rich reward if she could discover the secret of Samson's strength.

The next time Samson came to visit her, Delilah said, "If you really loved me, you would keep no secrets from me. What makes you so strong? Is it true that it is impossible to bind you with ropes?"

Samson laughed good-naturedly thinking that here was a chance for some good sport.

"If they bind me with seven fresh bowstrings that were never dried," replied Samson, "then I should become as weak as any other man."

When Samson was asleep, Delilah bound him with seven fresh bowstrings. The Philistines waited in an inner room.

"The Philistines are upon you, Samson," she shouted.

Samson stretched and tore the strings apart as one might tear a leaf.

SAMSON CARRYING AWAY THE GATES OF GAZA

"You have mocked me," said Delilah. "You did not tell me the truth."

Samson laughed. "Tie me with new ropes that have never been used."

That night Delilah bound him with new ropes and shouted, "The Philistines are upon you, Samson."

Samson stretched and broke the new ropes as if they were but a thread of cotton.

"Twice you have lied," said Delilah. "Why do you not tell me the truth?"

"Bind my hair with a strong pin so that it does not fall loosely over my shoulders," replied Samson. "Then I shall be like any other man."

Delilah bound Samson's hair. "The Philistines are upon you," she shouted.

Samson easily brushed the pin from his hair, and his hair fell loosely again over his shoulders.

"I see that you do not love me," said Delilah. "When two people are in love there can be no secrets between them. I promise that no harm shall come to you. But I cannot rest until you reveal this secret unto me."

At first Samson was silent, but Delilah grew more and more urgent. At last Samson weakened.

"As long as I keep my vow to God my strength will remain with me," said Samson. "I am a Nazarite. I do not touch strong drink, nor has my hair ever been cut. If I break my vow by cutting my hair then my strength will depart from me."

Delilah knew that this time Samson had told her the

truth. When Samson was asleep, a Philistine shaved off the hair of his head.

"The Philistines are upon you," shouted Delilah.

Samson awoke and thought to himself, "I shall free my-self as I did before."

He stretched, but his strength had departed from him. As soon as his vow was broken, he was no stronger than any ordinary person.

Samson was now a prisoner of the Philistines.

4. SAMSON'S DEATH

The Philistines treated Samson very cruelly. They put out both his eyes. Then they led the blind Samson to a prison in the city of Gaza where Samson had once walked away with the gates of the city.

In Gaza they bound Samson with chains of brass, and threw him into a dungeon.

Unhappy Samson knew that he was at fault. He had been a hero in strength, but not a hero in spirit. Because of his love for strange women he had broken his vow. Now his strength was gone.

Samson prayed to God for forgiveness.

Meanwhile Samson's hair began to grow back. Because of his change of heart, Samson's strength began to return to him little by little.

The Philistines rejoiced greatly over the capture of Samson. They thanked Dagon, a fish-god whom they worshiped.

"Let us offer a sacrifice to Dagon for he has delivered our enemy into our hands," they said joyfully.

Thousands of Philistines gathered for the sacrifice. They ate, drank and were merry.

"Call for Samson that he may make us sport," they shouted.

Samson was brought before the Philistines. They scorned and mocked the blind Samson.

"Look at the mighty Samson!" they laughed as they tortured him.

Samson turned to the boy who led him. "Let me rest against one of the pillows," he said. "I am very tired."

The lad brought him to one of the pillars.

And Samson prayed unto God, "O Lord God, remember me, I pray. Give me strength so that I may be avenged for the loss of my two eyes."

Samson then took hold of the two middle pillars upon which the Philistine temple rested. He put his right arm around one pillar, and his left arm around the other.

"Let me die with the Philistines," said Samson.

He bent with all his might. The pillars began to move.

"The roof is falling! The roof is falling!" shouted the Philistines.

It was too late. The temple crumbled killing the thousands who had come to make sport of Samson.

Samson's body was found among the ruins.

Samson was probably the strongest man who has ever lived. But he was not a great hero. The real hero must be great in character.

The book of Proverbs says, "He that rules his own spirit is greater than he who takes a city." Samson could capture a city but he could not rule his own spirit.

EXERCISES

I. True or false? (Review section 1, pages 75 to 78.)

1. Samson did not touch wine because drinking wine is forbidden by the Hebrew religion.
2. Samson killed a lion with his sword.
3. The parents were sad because Samson married a Philistine girl.
4. Samson burned the Philistine fields by putting torches between the tails of foxes that were tied together.
5. The Philistines rewarded Samson's father-in-law.

II. Fill in the correct name or phrase—Philistines or "men of Judah." (Review section 2, pages 78 to 79.)

1. The _____ wanted to kill Samson.
2. The _____ promised not to harm Samson.
3. Samson allowed the _____ to bind him.
4. Samson killed 1000 _____ with the jawbone of a donkey.
5. The _____ tried to capture Samson in Gaza, but he walked away with the gates of the city.

III. Answer each question in a complete sentence. (Review sections 3 and 4, pages 80 to 84.)

1. How long did Samson rule over Israel?
2. Who revealed Samson's secret to the Philistines?
3. What was the secret of Samson's strength?
4. Why did the Philistines gather in the temple of Dagon?
5. How did Samson destroy the temple?

IV. Questions for discussion:

1. "Samson and Delilah" was made into a successful

moving-picture. Why would an audience enjoy a picture based on this story?

2. In your opinion was Samson a hero?

REVIEW QUESTIONS

for Units One and Two (pages 17 to 86)

1. What did each of the following accomplish for Israel: Joshua, Deborah, Gideon, Samson?
2. Mention 3 important problems that the Israelites had to solve after the death of Moses. How did each of the leaders help solve these problems?
3. Write a sentence about each of the following: Eleazar, Phineas, Rahab, Barak, Sisera, Jael, Abimelech, Jotham, Ruth, Naomi, Boaz.
4. Mention the importance of each of the following: Jordan River, Jericho, Gilgal, Ai, Gibeon, Shiloh, Shechem, Mount Tabor, Kishon, Mount Gerizim, Gaza, Moab, Bethlehem.

TEST

on Units One and Two

I. Choose the correct name. (20 points)

1. _____ made a treaty of peace with Joshua. (Ai, Gibeon)
2. The ark rested in the city of _____. (Shechem, Shiloh)
3. _____ freed Israel from the enemy. (Deborah, Ruth)
4. _____ refused to be king. (Abimelech, Gideon)
5. Samson delivered Israel from the hand of the _____. (Midianites, Philistines)

II. Match: (20 points)

Column A	Column B
Bethlehem	1. Joshua's camp
Gaza	2. Joshua's first victory
Gilgal	3. Barak's camp
Jericho	4. Home of Naomi
Mount Tabor	5. Samson's prison

III. Why? (30 points)

1. Why did Joshua save the life of Rahab?
2. Why did the 2½ tribes set up a monument near the Jordan?
3. Why is Deborah compared to Joan of Arc?
4. Why is the story of Ruth read on Shavuot?
5. Why did Samson lose his strength when his hair was cut?

IV. True or false? (30 points)

1. Joshua defeated Jericho by means of an ambush.
2. The 2½ tribes received land west of the Jordan.
3. The Israelites were able to store water for the dry season because they lined the cisterns with water-proof lime plaster.
4. Barak refused to fight against Sisera without Deborah's help.
5. The farmers celebrated the barley harvest on Sukkot.
6. Ruth's reward was that David, Israel's greatest king, was descended from her.
7. Poor people were allowed to glean after the reapers.
8. Gideon defeated the Midianites because he had a large army.
9. Jotham said that Abimelech was like a fig-tree.
10. Samson destroyed the temple of Dagon even though he was blind.

UNIT THREE

The Beginning of the Kingdom

CHAPTER VIII

SAMUEL

1. THE BIRTH OF SAMUEL

THERE LIVED an Israelite in the hill-country of Ephraim named Elkanah.

Each year Elkanah would go up to Shiloh to worship before God and to offer a sacrifice.

Now Elkanah had two wives, one named Hannah and one named Peninnah. Each year Elkanah would give Peninnah and her children portions of the sacrifice.

To Hannah he would give a double portion for he loved her dearly. But Hannah had no children. She wept and would not eat.

And Elkanah said, "Hannah, why do you weep? And why do you not eat? And why are you sad?"

"If only we were blessed with children!" wept Hannah.

Then Hannah would sadly rise and pray to God. And it came to pass that Eli, the High Priest, saw her pray to God. Hannah's prayer came from her heart. Her lips moved but her voice could not be heard.

For a moment Eli thought that she had drunk too much wine.

"Put away your wine," said Eli. "This is a house of worship."

Hannah sadly answered, "I have not partaken of any wine. I am a woman of sorrowful spirit, for God has not blessed me with any children."

And Eli said, "Go in peace, and may the God of Israel grant that your prayer be answered."

Hannah's prayer was answered! Elkanah and Hannah were blessed with a son whom they called Samuel, meaning "God has heard."

When Samuel was a few years old, Hannah brought him to Shiloh.

And Hannah said to Eli, "I am the woman who stood near you praying unto God. And God has answered my prayer and blessed me with a son. And now, in thanksgiving, I have brought the child here to serve before God."

Eli blessed Hannah who returned to her home. And the child Samuel served in the house of God in Shiloh.

2. SAMUEL'S DREAM

As Samuel grew, Eli taught him the laws of Moses. Samuel watched as the kind Eli judged the people and as he served in the house of God.

Each year Hannah came to Shiloh bringing with her a new robe for the child. She was pleased to see how he grew from year to year.

When Samuel grew a little older he was shocked to

learn that Eli's two sons were not kind and good like their father. The presents that were brought to the house of worship in Shiloh they would take for themselves. They would eat the food without carrying out the sacrifices properly. They mistreated the men and women who came to Shiloh.

One day Eli said to his sons, "I have heard many evil reports concerning you. God will not forgive you if you continue to sin."

Eli's rebuke was so gentle, however, that his sons did not take it to heart.

Once when the child Samuel lay down to sleep he heard a voice calling, "Samuel, Samuel."

Samuel quickly rose from his bed, ran to Eli and said, "Here am I. Why did you call?"

Eli was surprised. "I did not call. Lie down again."

A second time Samuel heard a voice calling, "Samuel, Samuel."

Again he ran to Eli saying, "Here am I."

"You are mistaken, my child," said Eli. "I did not call."

When this happened a third time, Eli said to Samuel, "Surely the Lord has appeared unto you. Return and listen to the word of God."

The child heard the voice call a fourth time, "Samuel, Samuel."

And Samuel replied, "Speak, O Lord, for Your servant listens."

And the voice of God said, "Because of the evil of the sons of Eli, I shall bring punishment upon the house of Eli.

And I shall remove the priesthood from his house and give it to another who is more faithful."

In the morning Samuel rose to open the doors of the house of God. He was afraid, however, to tell Eli of God's words.

But Eli called Samuel saying, "Samuel, my son."

And he said, "Here am I."

And Eli asked, "What were the words of God? Hide nothing, I pray you."

Samuel repeated word for word what he had heard.

Eli sadly said, "May the will of God be done."

As Samuel grew all Israel heard of his wisdom. From the city of Dan in the north to the city of Beersheba in the south, all praised Samuel, the servant of the Lord.

3. THE ARK OF GOD

After the death of Samson the struggle between the Philistines and the Israelites had become more and more severe.

There was a pitched battle between the Philistines and Israel in which the Philistines were the victors. About 4000 Israelites were slain in battle.

When the soldiers returned to their camp they asked, "Why has God permitted us to be defeated? Let us fetch the ark of God out of Shiloh and bring it with us to the battle."

The sons of Eli brought the ark with them from Shiloh to the battle-front. When the soldiers saw the ark they shouted with a great shout.

The Philistines, hearing the noise, asked, "What is the meaning of this shouting?"

At first they were greatly afraid when they heard that the ark, containing the two tablets of stone, had been brought to the battle-front.

"Woe unto us! Who will deliver us from their mighty God?" they asked.

But their officers urged them to fight bravely.

"Be strong," they said, "or you will be servants unto Israel, just as they were servants unto you."

The Philistines fought bravely and defeated Israel. Eli's two sons were killed on the field of battle and the ark of God was captured by the Philistines.

Eli waited eagerly in Shiloh for news from the battle-front. A refugee from the battle ran quickly to Shiloh with the sad news.

"What news, my son?" asked Eli with trembling heart.

"Israel has fled," replied the refugee. "There has been a great slaughter, and both your sons died bravely on the battlefield."

"And the ark of God?" asked Eli anxiously.

"The ark has been captured," replied the refugee.

At mention of the capture of the ark of God, Eli fell backward and died.

It was a sad day for Israel. The people tore their garments and put earth upon their heads as a sign of mourning. A grandson of Eli's who was born on the day of the defeat was called "Ichabod," which means "The glory has departed."

People no longer came to Shiloh now that the ark had been captured. The temple in which Eli served fell into ruins. The priesthood passed forever from the house of Eli.

The Philistines did not keep the ark very long. Soon after the ark had been captured a plague broke out in the Philistine cities.

"The God of Israel is sending against us the plagues that were visited on Egypt," they cried in fright.

The Philistines placed the ark on a cart drawn by two cows. The cows were led to the crossroads, from which three roads branched out.

The cows, of their own accord, followed the road which led into the hill-country of Israel.

The Israelites rejoiced to receive back the ark of God. A family of Levites was placed in charge of the ark which contained the precious tablets of stone on which were written the ten commandments.

4. SAMUEL—JUDGE OF A UNITED NATION

At this sad moment in the history of Israel the 12 tribes turned to Samuel to be their judge and ruler.

Samuel's first task was to unite the 12 tribes. Never since the death of Joshua had the tribes really been united. Even Deborah, one of the greatest of the Judges, succeeded in uniting only about half of the tribes.

There had been many civil wars among the tribes. The tribe of Benjamin was almost wiped out in such a war.

Once, before the days of Samuel, the tribe of Ephraim

fought against the 2½ tribes. Since all Israelites spoke the same language and looked alike, neither side could tell friend from foe.

The 2½ tribes, however, picked the word "shibboleth," which means "a stream," as the password. The men of Ephraim found it hard to pronounce "sh." Instead of "shibboleth" they said "sibboleth."

When an Ephraimite was caught as a prisoner, he would try to pass as a member of the 2½ tribes. He would be asked to pronounce "shibboleth". If he said "sibboleth" his captors knew he was from the tribe of Ephraim, and he would be kept as a prisoner. (Because of this incident "shibboleth" is now used in English to mean "a password".)

The tribes loved Samuel so dearly that they obeyed his words at all times. Thus the tribes became united once more.

Samuel picked a city in each section to which he would go to judge the people. From Dan in the north to Beer-sheba in the south, people brought their problems to Samuel.

After he had visited each city Samuel would return to Ramah, the city in which he had been born, and where he made his home.

Samuel's second task was to make the people worship God and put away their idols. Samuel called the men of Israel together to the city of Mizpah.

And Samuel said, "If you wish to return to God with all your hearts, then put away the idols and the false gods."

And the people said, "We have sinned. We will worship the one true God."

Never had there been such a gathering since the days of Joshua.

The Philistines heard that Samuel had gathered the children of Israel to Mizpah.

"They plan to rebel against us," said the Philistines.

Quickly they sent an army against Mizpah.

In terror the Israelites turned to Samuel. "Pray to God to save us," they begged.

An army of Israelites was quickly formed.

What happened in the days of Deborah over a hundred years before happened again. The stars in their courses fought against the Philistines.

First the earth began to tremble beneath the Philistines. Then great clouds appeared in the skies. A storm broke loose. The tents of the Philistines were lifted by the wind and carried away. Thunderbolts were heard.

By the glare of the lightning the Israelites could see the Philistine soldiers flee in terror.

The united tribes were able to form a strong army under the leadership of Samuel. Israel was united and free once more.

EXERCISES

I. Who said to whom? (Review sections 1 and 2, pages 89 to 92.)
   1. "Why do you weep? And why do you not eat?"
   2. "I am a woman of sorrowful spirit, for God has not blessed me with any children."

3. "I have heard many evil reports concerning you. God will not forgive you if you continue to sin."
4. "Because of the evil of the sons of Eli, I shall bring punishment upon the house of Eli."
5. "What were the words of God? Hide nothing, I pray you."

II. Choose the correct name or phrase. (Review section 3, pages 92 to 94.)
   1. The Israelites brought the ark from (a—Gilgal; b—Shechem; c—Shiloh).
   2. The ark was brought by (a—Eli; b—Samuel; c—the sons of Eli).
   3. Israel was defeated by the (a—Canaanites; b—Midianites; c—Philistines).
   4. Eli died (a—when he heard the sad news; b—as a prisoner of war; c—on the field of battle).
   5. The Philistines returned the ark because (a—they received ransom money; b—plagues broke out in their cities; c—they made peace with Israel).

III. Arrange in the order in which these events happened. (Review section 4, pages 94 to 96.)
   1. The Philistines fled in terror because of an earthquake and storm.
   2. There were many civil wars among the tribes.
   3. The Israelites said to Samuel, "We have sinned. We will worship the one true God."
   4. Samuel was made judge.
   5. The Philistines sent an army against Mizpah.
   6. Samuel called the people of Israel together to the city of Mizpah.

IV. Questions for discussion:
   1. Eli was partly at fault for the bad character of his

two sons because he was afraid to scold them. How strict should a parent be?

2. What problems faced Samuel as judge of Israel? How did he solve these problems?

THINGS TO DO

1. *Holiday Scrap-book*—The story of Samuel's birth is read in the synagogue on Rosh Ha-Shanah. Since Rosh Ha-Shanah marks the birth of the world, we read of the birth of great men like Isaac and Samuel.

Start a holiday scrap-book in which you will draw pictures for each holiday. For Rosh Ha-Shanah you might draw a New Year greeting card, a *shofar*, or a picture of the child Samuel.

2. *The Ark*—Visit your synagogue and examine the holy ark *(aron kodesh)*. Note the scrolls of the law in the ark, the ten commandments above the ark, and the *ner tamid*, or eternal light, in front of the ark.

Draw a picture of the ark.

PUZZLE

Substitute 3-letter words for each of the following phrases. The words will be identical whether read *across* or *down*.

1. A High Priest who served in Shiloh
2. Abraham's nephew
3. The initials of "Israel's Twelve Tribes"

CHAPTER IX

SAUL—ISRAEL'S FIRST KING

1. "GIVE US A KING"

WHEN SAMUEL was old he made his sons judges. But his sons were not good judges for they took bribes.

The elders of Israel came to Samuel and said, "Behold, you are old. Your sons do not walk in your ways. Give us a king to rule over us so that we may be like all the other nations."

Samuel was very angry. "God rules over us. Why do you need a king?"

"We need a king to rule, and to judge."

Samuel prayed to God for guidance. And the Lord said, "Warn them of what will happen when they select a king. If they do not wish to heed your warning, then appoint a king to rule over them."

Samuel then said to the people, "This will be the manner of the king that will reign over you. He will take your sons to drive his chariots and to be his horsemen. He will appoint them as captains of thousands, and captains of fifties. He will force them to plow his ground, to reap his harvest, and to make his weapons.

"He will take your daughters to be perfumers, and to be cooks and to be bakers. And he will take your fields, and your vineyards, and your olive-yards, and give them to his servants.

"And he will take your men-servants, and your maid-servants, and your cattle and donkeys, and put them to his work.

"He will take the tenth of your flocks, and you will be his servants. And you will cry out in that day because of your king whom you have chosen, but the Lord will not answer you on that day."

But the people would not listen to the words of Samuel.

"We must have a king," they pleaded. "In time of peace he will judge us. In time of war he will lead us into battle. If we do not have a king our enemies will destroy us."

And Samuel said, "I shall pray to God to find us a king who will rule justly over us. Meanwhile, return to your cities."

2. SAUL, THE SON OF KISH

Now there was a man of the tribe of Benjamin whose name was Kish. He had a son named Saul who was brave and strong. From his shoulders and upward he was taller than any of the other people.

Once the donkeys belonging to Kish wandered away.

And Kish said to Saul, "Take one of the servants with you and arise, go seek the donkeys."

Saul and his servant searched in the hill-country of Benjamin and of Ephraim. The donkeys were nowhere to be found.

At last Saul said to his servant, "Let us return or my father will be worried about us."

"Samuel is visiting this city today," replied the servant. "Let us go to him. Perhaps he can help us."

"Well said," agreed Saul. "Let us go to find him."

Meanwhile, the word of God had come to Samuel saying, "Tomorrow, about this time, I shall send you a man of the tribe of Benjamin whom you will anoint as king. He will deliver the children of Israel from the hand of the Philistines, for I have heard Israel's cry of distress."

The next day when Saul approached, Samuel recognized immediately that this was the man chosen to be king.

"I have come to you for help," said Saul. "A flock of donkeys belonging to my father has wandered away. Perhaps you can advise us."

"Do not worry about the donkeys," replied Samuel. "They have been found. There is a sacrifice in the city today. Come with me, for a place of honor is reserved for you."

"A place of honor? I am of the tribe of Benjamin, the smallest of the tribes. And my family is the least of the families of Benjamin. Surely, you have made some mistake."

"There is no mistake. Come with me," repeated Samuel.

Saul in amazement took his place next to Samuel at the banquet where thirty nobles of Israel were gathered.

Samuel arranged for lodging for the night for Saul. The next day at dawn, Samuel said to Saul, "The donkeys you have sought have been returned to your father. But I have something more important to tell you. The word of God has come to me to anoint you king over Israel."

Samuel then took a bottle of oil, and anointed Saul by pouring drops of oil on Saul's head.

"God has chosen you to be His anointed", said Samuel. "Rule wisely and justly, and serve God with a pure heart."

Samuel then gathered the elders of Israel to Mizpah.

"You have done a foolish thing to ask for a king," said Samuel. "But now I shall show you whom God has chosen —one of the people who will rule wisely over the people."

Samuel then called Saul to step forward. Saul, however, was so bashful that he was found hiding amidst the baggage.

When Saul came forward the people saw that in appearance Saul was kingly indeed, for he stood head and shoulders above all others.

"Long live King Saul!" they shouted. "Long live King Saul!"

3. KING SAUL

Not all the children of Israel accepted Saul as king. Some of the nobles were angry because a member of an unimportant family had been chosen king.

"How can this man save us?" they mocked.

Samuel advised Saul to return to his home until an opportunity came to prove he deserved to be king. Then he would be crowned king.

Saul, the king, returned to his farm and to his oxen.

Soon thereafter Nahash, king of the Ammonites, attacked the city of Jabesh in the land of Gilead. This was one of the sections east of the Jordon settled by the 2 ½ tribes.

"Make a treaty of peace with us," said the men of Jabesh, "and we shall be your servants."

"But first I shall blind each person's right eye," replied Nahash.

In horror the men of Gilead sent messengers to the twelve tribes of Israel calling for help.

The messenger to the tribe of Benjamin found Saul following the oxen. When Saul heard of the threat by Nahash, he grew very angry.

Saul cut a team of oxen into many pieces. He sent messengers to each section of Israel saying, "Thus shall be done to the oxen of any man who does not follow Saul and Samuel."

From every city of Israel men gathered behind the banner of Saul.

Saul sent word to the city of Jabesh. "Tomorrow, before noon when the sun is high in the heavens, you will be delivered from the enemy."

Saul kept his word. The Israelites attacked at dawn. By noon there was no trace left of the Ammonite army.

Israel rejoiced at this brilliant victory by their new king.

"Where are the men who mocked our new king? Let them be put to death!" shouted the people.

"They have my full pardon," said Saul. "Let no Israelite be harmed on this great day."

Samuel then ordered Israel to Gilgal, where Joshua's camp once stood, to crown Saul king.

After Saul had been made king, Samuel delivered his farewell address.

"All my life I have served you," said Samuel. "If any man can say I have wronged him, let him step forward. Whose ox have I taken? Whom have I cheated? From whom have I taken a bribe? Whom have I oppressed?"

"You have never wronged any of us," cried the Israelites.

"Let God and His anointed, Saul, be witness," said Samuel.

"He is witness! He is witness!" repeated the people.

"Now I take my farewell," said Samuel. "Remember this. If you deal wickedly then God will sweep away both you and your king. But serve the Lord in truth and with pure hearts, and God will bless both you and the royal family."

4. JONATHAN, THE SON OF SAUL

One of the reasons that the people had demanded a king was that the Philistines had regained the upper hand when Samuel grew old.

There were Philistine garrisons in many parts of the country. The Philistines did not permit any blacksmiths to dwell among the Israelites for fear that the Israelites might make swords and spears.

After Saul had been king for two years his son, Jonathan, attacked the Philistine garrison in Geba.

Jonathan won an easy victory over the small band of Philistine soldiers in Geba.

"Let us destroy this new king before he becomes too strong," said the Philistine lords.

The Philistines gathered a tremendous army. They sent thousands of chariots, of horsemen and of foot-soldiers against Israel.

Many of the soldiers in the Philistine army were from foreign tribes. The Philistines forced prisoners to fight for them. There were even Israelites whom they forced to fight in their army.

When the people of Israel saw the size of the Philistine army they trembled. Very few of Saul's soldiers had even swords or spears.

"It was easy for Saul to defeat Nahash," they said, "for he was only a desert bandit. But how can Saul fight against this great army?"

Saul's army began to dwindle away in fear. Many fled from Saul's camp at Gilgal over the Jordan River. Others hid in caves and in pits, or behind rocks and thickets.

One day Jonathan said to his armor-bearer, "Let us go up to the Philistine camp. Maybe we can catch a few prisoners."

Jonathan said nothing to Saul. He and the armor-bearer walked silently along a narrow pass through the mountains. There above them on the mountain crag was the outpost of the Philistine camp.

"Gideon once destroyed a whole army with a few men," said Jonathan. "Maybe we can do the same."

"I'll go with you," responded the brave armor-bearer.

"Let's stand at the foot of the crag," said Jonathan, "where the enemy can see us. If they shout, 'Stay there and we'll show you a thing or two', then we will stay where we are and not go farther. But if they say, 'Come up to us, if you dare', then it is a sign that we can go up and conquer."

As soon as the Philistines on top of the crag saw the two Hebrews at the foot of the mountain, they began to shout, "Why don't you come up to us, you cowards?"

"That is just the sign for which we have been waiting," Jonathan called out to his companion. "Follow me."

On hands and knees Jonathan and his armor-bearer slowly climbed up the steep rock.

The Philistines, unable to see them, laughed.

"We frightened them away," they said.

It took some time for Jonathan and the armor-bearer to climb to the top. Nobody suspected their approach. Before them was an outpost of twenty soldiers.

"Death to the Philistines!" shouted Jonathan.

Hurling huge rocks at the surprised enemy, Jonathan and his companion wiped out nearly the whole group before they could resist.

"Flee!" shouted one of the Philistines. "Flee for your lives! The Hebrews have command of the mountain top!"

Little did they know that two men were attacking a whole army.

A surprising thing then happened. The foreign soldiers had no love for the Philistines. Fearing for their lives they turned their swords against the Philistines. The Israelites who had been forced to fight for the Philistines did the same.

The Philistines fled in terror. To add to the confusion so many rocks were loosened by the fleeing soldiers, there was almost a landslide.

Saul's camp watched in amazement as the Philistines fled from before an imaginary enemy. After numbering his small army, Saul discovered Jonathan's absence.

"God has given us victory," declared Saul. "Death to the man who tastes food before we avenge ourselves on our enemy!"

Quickly the Israelites pursued after the Philistines. They were joined by many who had been hiding in caves.

They pursued the enemy as far as Aijalon, where Joshua had once commanded the sun to stand still. Saul won a great victory.

Jonathan, not hearing his father's vow, tasted some honey that he found in the forest.

Saul in dismay said, "What have you done? Even though you are my son I must carry out my vow."

"Let no harm come to Jonathan," shouted the people. "He did not hear your vow. Through him God has sent us victory."

"You are witness that I have not broken my vow," replied Saul.

Thus Jonathan was rescued from death by the people.

And all Israel praised Saul and Jonathan, the heroes of this glorious victory.

EXERCISES

I. Why? (Review sections 1 and 2, pages 99 to 102.)

1. Why were the people not pleased with Samuel's sons?
2. Why was Samuel angry when the people asked for a king?
3. Why did the people insist that they wanted a king in spite of Samuel's warning?
4. Why did Saul go to Samuel?
5. Why was Saul chosen to be king?

II. Complete each sentence. (Review section 3, pages 102 to 104.)

JABESH, NAHASH, NOBLES, SAMUEL, SAUL

1. The _____ refused to accept Saul as king.
2. The city of _____ wanted to make peace with the Ammonites.
3. _____ threatened to blind each person's right eye.
4. _____ defeated the Ammonites.
5. _____ in his farewell address called God to witness that he had not wronged a single Israelite.

III. True or false? (Review section 4, pages 104 to 107.)

1. The Philistines did not permit any smiths to dwell among the Israelites.
2. Jonathan wiped out the garrison in Geba.
3. The Philistines had many foreign soldiers.
4. The Philistine camp was in a valley.
5. Samuel led a surprise attack against the Philistines.

IV. Questions for discussion:

1. Why is Samuel considered the greatest of the Judges?
2. Do you think that the Israelites were right in demanding a king?

3. In 1948 the new State of Israel picked a president instead of a king. Do you think that they made the right decision? Why?

THINGS TO DO

1. *Class Mural*—Plan a mural as a term project. The following subjects might be included: shepherds in ancient Israel; farm life; the walls of Jericho; Canaanite chariots; the trees in Jotham's fable; Ruth gleaning after the reapers; Samuel anointing Saul.

2. *Council of the Twelve Tribes*—Pretend you are representatives of the twelve tribes. Debate the question of whether Israel should choose a king or not. Select a leader to play the part of Samuel.

LAST LETTER FIRST—A GAME

Start with a proper name taken from Jewish history. The next student must select a name beginning with the letter with which the previous name ended. For example: if the first student selects "Isaac," the next person can pick "Canaan," etc.

CHAPTER X

DAVID,
THE SHEPHERD HERO

1. DAVID IS ANOINTED

AT FIRST Samuel was greatly pleased with Saul. The new king fought bravely against Israel's enemies, and ruled the people wisely.

But soon Samuel was displeased with Saul's actions. Once Samuel agreed to offer a sacrifice to God before Saul went into battle. Saul did not wait for Samuel but offered the sacrifice himself although he was not trained as a priest.

Samuel once ordered Saul to punish the wicked Amalekites and to slay their king. When Israel left Egypt the Amalekites attacked the weak refugees who had just escaped from slavery. Often the Amalekites would raid the borders of Israel and kill as many as they could.

Saul defeated the Amalekites, but taking pity on the king kept him as a prisoner.

Samuel in anger said, "Just as his sword has made

women childless, so shall his mother be made childless."
The wicked king of the Amalekites was then put to death.

Although Saul was too lenient with the king of the
Amalekites, he was too severe with others. Saul was afraid
that the men of Gibeon might some day turn against
Israel. He therefore treated them very harshly.

This was a great sin for he broke the vow that Joshua
had made of lasting peace between Israel and Gibeon.

Sometimes Saul became very sad and moody. At other
times a fit of madness would seize him, and Saul would
do foolish things.

At last the word of God came to Samuel saying, "Because Saul has not obeyed my voice, anoint another to be
king of Israel. Go to Bethlehem, and there anoint one of
the sons of Jesse."

Samuel went to Bethlehem and invited the elders of the
city to a special sacrifice.

Samuel then turned to the house of Jesse.

"You and your sons," said Samuel, "must attend the
sacrifice. Call your sons before me so that I might know
them."

Jesse called his oldest son, Eliab, before Samuel. The
prophet Samuel was greatly pleased when he saw a tall,
strong, handsome young man. He looked kind and wise.

And Samuel thought, "Surely he will make a worthy
king."

But the word of God came to Samuel, "He is not the
Lord's anointed. Man judges by the outward appearance.
But God looks into a person's heart."

Samuel then asked Jesse to bring his second son forward.

Again word came from God. "He is not the Lord's anointed."

After Jesse had introduced seven sons, Samuel asked, "Are these all your sons?"

"I have one more son, my youngest," replied Jesse. "But he is taking care of the sheep."

"Let him, too, come to the sacrifice," said Samuel. "We shall wait until he comes."

Jesse sent for his youngest son, David. When David appeared before Samuel, he heard the word of God, "He will be My anointed."

Jesse and his sons sat next to Samuel at the sacrifice.

Samuel called David aside and anointed him with oil.

"After the death of Saul, you will be king," said Samuel. "Let this remain a secret between us. When you become king, judge the people with kindness, and worship God with a pure heart."

David in amazement returned to his sheep to think about Samuel's words.

2. GOLIATH OF GATH

David soon had his first chance to visit the court of Saul.

Saul's servants said, "Music will drive away sadness. Let us find a man who can play on the harp to comfort Saul."

"I know a young shepherd who is very skillful in play-

DAVID THE SHEPHERD

ing," said one of the servants. "His name is David, the son of Jesse."

Saul agreed to invite David to the court. Whenever a spirit of sadness came over Saul, young David would play and Saul was comforted.

The members of the court liked David very much. Prince Jonathan, especially, was attracted to the young shepherd.

One day a messenger ran to Saul's court.

"The Philistines! The Philistines are attacking!" he shouted.

Quickly Saul assembled his army. David, meanwhile, returned to Bethlehem since he was too young to fight.

The Israelites encamped on a high mountain. Opposite them on another mountain were the Philistines. A valley separated the two mountains from each other.

From the Philistine camp there strode forth a great giant, named Goliath, of the city of Gath. He had a helmet of brass upon his head, and he wore a heavy coat of mail. He carried a great javelin. His shield-bearer walked before him carrying his shield.

Goliath of Gath stood midway between the two camps.

And he cried unto the army of Israel, "Why do you prepare for battle? Choose a man as your champion, and let him come down to me. If he can kill me, then we shall be your servants. But if I defeat him, then you will be our servants and will serve us."

When the Israelite soldiers saw Goliath they were greatly afraid.

"I challenge the army of Israel this day," called out Goliath. "Give me a man that we may fight together. I defy Israel!"

The Israelites, however, remained silent. Goliath came forth each day, hurling insults at the army of Israel. But there was no champion who felt strong enough to enter into combat with Goliath.

One day Jesse said to David, "Three of your brothers are in Saul's camp. Bring them corn, and bread, and cheese so that they will have food to eat. Go and find out whether all is well with them."

David rejoiced at the chance to visit the battle-front. As he spoke to his brothers, Goliath again came forward.

"Where are your brave men?" mocked Goliath. "Send your champion to fight me. I defy Israel!"

David turned to one of the soldiers and asked, "What is the reward for the man who kills this boastful giant?"

"King Saul has promised great riches to the champion who defeats Goliath," replied the soldier.

"His beautiful daughter will be given in marriage to the champion," added another soldier.

David's brother, Eliab, overheard the conversation.

"Why don't you go back to your sheep?" asked Eliab angrily. "I know how bold you are. You think that you're a soldier and would like to fight. Why don't you go back to Bethlehem before you get hurt?"

David did not reply to his brother, but quietly approaching one of the captains he said, "Send word to the king that I am willing to fight Goliath."

3. DAVID AND GOLIATH

King Saul was very much surprised when he heard that his musician, the shepherd David, wanted to fight the giant.

"How can you fight against this Philistine?" Saul asked. "You are but a youth, and Goliath is a mighty man of war."

Then David replied, "God will protect me. Once when I took care of my father's sheep, a lion came and caught a sheep. With my shepherd's staff I delivered the sheep from the lion. When the lion attacked I slew the lion. At another time a bear attacked the flock and I slew the bear. God who saved me from the paw of the lion and the paw of the bear, will deliver me out of the hand of this Philistine."

"Go," said Saul, "and may God be with you."

Saul clothed David with a helmet of brass and a coat of mail. But David could hardly move so heavy were the helmet and the coat of mail.

"I do not need these," said David as he removed the helmet and the mail. "My shepherd's staff is enough."

David then chose five smooth stones from the brook and put them into his shepherd's bag.

David descended into the valley to meet Goliath. The giant came nearer and nearer, his shield-bearer walking before him.

Goliath grew furious with anger when he saw David.

"Am I a dog," he shouted, "that they send a boy

against me with a stick? I will give your flesh to the birds of the air, and to the beasts of the field!"

Then David replied, "You come to me with a sword and with a spear, but I come to you in the name of the God of Israel. I will smite you this day so that all will know that the battle is the Lord's even without sword and spear."

Goliath approached to do battle with David. The shepherd quickly put his hand in his bag, took out a smooth stone and placed it in his sling-shot.

David took aim and then let fly. The stone sailed through the air and found its mark. It sank deep into the giant's forehead.

Goliath fell to the ground unconscious. David ran to the fallen giant. He drew the Philistine's sword from its sheath, and killed Goliath with the giant's own sword.

When the Philistines saw that their champion was dead they fled in terror. The Israelites followed in hot pursuit, and defeated the Philistines.

David, the youthful shepherd, was the hero of the day.

EXERCISES

I. Match. (Review section 1, pages 110 to 112.)

Column A	Column B
David	1. Defeated Amalekites
Eliab	2. Shepherd
Jesse	3. Arranged sacrifice in Bethlehem
Joshua	4. Father of 8 sons
Samuel	5. Made treaty with Gibeonites
Saul	6. Oldest son

II. Answer each question in a complete sentence. (Review section 2, pages 112 to 115.)

1. Why did David go to Saul's court?
2. How did Goliath challenge Israel?
3. Why did Jesse send David to the battlefield?
4. What reward did King Saul promise to the one who defeated Goliath?
5. Why was Eliab angry at David?

III. Fill in the correct name—David or Goliath. (Review section 3, pages 116 to 117.)

1. _____ saved a sheep from being killed by a lion.
2. _____ removed the helmet and coat of mail.
3. _____ said, "Am I a dog that they send a boy against me with a stick?"
4. _____ used a sling-shot.
5. David killed the giant with the sword of _____.

IV. Questions for discussion:

2. Who was more important—King Saul or the prophet, Samuel?
3. Compare the life of a shepherd in the days of David with the life of a shepherd in Israel today.

THINGS TO DO

1. *Chart*—Construct a chart listing 10 heroes of Israel from the time of Abraham to the time of David. Next to each name, tell why the leader is famous or what he did for the Hebrew people.

2. *Broadcast*—Arrange a "We were there" broadcast for the David and Goliath fight. The broadcaster might interview King Saul, Jonathan, Hebrew soldiers, David, Eliab, Goliath, the shield-bearer, Philistine soldiers.

A MAGIC SQUARE

Fill in the correct number for each square. All columns, vertical, horizontal and diagonal, should add up to 15.

a	b	c
d	e	f
g	h	i

a. Jesse had _____ sons.

b. _____ daughter-in-law returned to Bethlehem with Naomi.

c. Deborah led half of the tribes of Israel, or _____ in all, against Sisera.

d. _____ of David's brothers were in Saul's army.

e. David picked _____ stones from the brook.

f. There are _____ letters in the name of the Philistine giant.

g. There are _____ letters in the name of the first king of Israel.

h. "Thou shalt have no other gods besides Me" is the first commandment. There are _____ other commandments.

i. There were _____ tablets of stone in the ark.

CHAPTER XI

SAUL AND DAVID

1. SAUL'S JEALOUSY

DAVID now remained at Saul's court as a soldier. He also played the harp when a spirit of sadness came over the king.

David was so brave that King Saul soon put him in charge of the entire army. And Israel was pleased with David.

Jonathan and David became loyal friends. The Bible tells us that "Jonathan loved him as his own soul." As a sign of friendship, Jonathan gave David his sword and his bow as a gift.

One day, as the army of Israel returned from a victorious battle against the Philistines, the women of Israel came out to greet the brave soldiers. They came with timbrels and with lyres, with singing and with dancing.

And the women sang:

"Saul has slain his thousands,
And David his ten thousands "

Saul became very angry when he heard this song.

"They have praised David more than me," said Saul. "Soon they will say that he deserves to be king!"

From that day on Saul hated David.

On the next day as David played his harp before Saul, a spirit of madness came over the king.

"Now is my chance to remove this dangerous young man," thought Saul.

He raised his spear and hurled it at David. But David nimbly stepped aside, and the spear pierced the wall.

The king's servants asked for David's pardon saying that a sudden craze had come over the king.

Saul now planned David's death in another way. As victor over Goliath, young David should have married Saul's daughter. Saul, however, demanded new victories against the Philistines as proof that David deserved to be his son-in-law.

"Maybe he will fall in battle," thought Saul. "Then I shall not be guilty of shedding his blood."

David, however, always returned victorious.

"Let me marry your daughter, Michal," said David to Saul, "for I love her. All that you have asked me to do I have done. And God has made me victorious over the Philistines."

Saul at last consented to the marriage. Saul's daughter, Michal, loved David.

There was great rejoicing on the day of the wedding, but in his heart Saul planned to kill David.

"I must find a way to kill David," thought the king.

2. DAVID AND JONATHAN

Saul now began to hint openly to his servants that he wanted David killed.

Jonathan warned David as soon as he discovered his father's wicked plans.

"There are rumors that my father plans to kill you," said Jonathan to David. "I believe that this is but a passing madness. Hide until I can gain more information.

The next day Jonathan spoke to Saul.

"My father, I plead with you, do not harm David. You rejoiced when he slew Goliath and saved Israel. Why then do you seek to shed innocent blood?"

Saul was moved by Jonathan's words.

"By God," swore Saul, "David will not be put to death. Tell him to return for no harm will befall him."

David returned and once more served as head of the army. Again he fought the Philistines, and conquered.

Some time passed. Once as David played the harp before Saul, another fit of madness came over the king. Again Saul lifted his spear and hurled it at David. As the spear whizzed by, David stepped aside just in time to avoid being hit.

David returned to his home. That night his wife, Michal, warned him, "I am afraid the house is being watched. If you delay any longer my father's messengers may arrest you."

David escaped through a rear window and fled to the home of Samuel, the prophet.

"Saul will not dare harm me as long as I take refuge with Samuel," thought David.

David guessed right. Saul came to Samuel's house planning to kill David. As soon as Saul heard the voice of Samuel, the spirit of God came over Saul. He began to recite verses in praise of God, warning the people to follow the laws of God.

"Is Saul, too, among the prophets?" asked the people in amazement.

Saul was sorry for the wrong he had intended to do. Meekly he returned to his court without harming David.

David rejoiced at his escape. But would Saul change his mind again? David arranged a secret meeting with Jonathan to ask for his advice.

Jonathan was happy to see David and again swore lasting friendship.

"Let us wait until tomorrow when the princes gather for the festival of the new month," said David. "Let me know what your father says when he sees that I am not present."

"If he speaks kindly then I am sure that his anger has passed," replied Jonathan. "If he speaks harshly then it is dangerous for you to return to the court."

"How can you let me know what your father has said?" asked David.

"Hide in the field," advised Jonathan. "I shall pretend that I am practicing archery. I shall shoot three arrows. When my armor-bearer looks for the arrows I shall wave with my hand. If I wave to the lad, 'Go farther', then you will know that the king seeks your life, and you will run farther and flee.

"But if I motion to the lad as if to say, 'Come back; you have gone too far'—then it is a sign that you can come back to the court."

When Saul saw that David was not present at the feast, he turned angrily to Jonathan and asked, "Where is your good friend, David? Does he not know that all members of the court attend the feast of the new month?"

Jonathan gave some excuse for David's absence.

"You fool!" raged Saul. "Have you no shame? As long as David lives, you will not succeed to the throne. Send for him for he deserves to die!"

"What has he done to deserve death?" demanded Jonathan.

When Saul placed his hand on the spear as if to hurl it at his son, Jonathan quickly left the banquet table.

He went to the field and shot several arrows. His armorbearer ran to retrieve the arrows.

"Farther! Farther!" called out Jonathan. "The arrows flew much farther."

David, alas, knew that Saul still planned to kill him, and that he must flee for his life.

When the lad had gathered all the arrows, David looked hither and thither. Seeing nobody who could spy on them, David ran to say farewell to Jonathan.

"Fear not," said Jonathan. "The hand of Saul, my father, will not find you. I know, too, that God has chosen you to be king over Israel. I shall be proud to be second to you."

"I swear that I will always deal kindly with you and your family," said David, "as you have dealt with me. Never has any man found a friend as loyal as you have been."

They said farewell. Jonathan returned to the court and David fled for his life.

3. SAUL PURSUES DAVID

Saul's hatred now knew no limits. He pursued David throughout the borders of Israel.

Anybody who helped David with food or with lodging was put to death by Saul.

The Philistines rejoiced that David and Saul were now enemies. The king of Gath invited David to his city.

When the Philistines saw David in Gath they cried out, "Put this man to death! This is the man who killed Goliath."

David quickly pretended that he was insane. He scribbled on the floor. He made wild motions. His hair was unkempt, and saliva ran down his beard.

"The man is mad!" exclaimed the king. "Do we not have enough madmen of our own that you bring another to the palace?"

Thinking him mad, the Philistines released David who quickly returned to Israel.

David now hid in the wilderness of Ziph in the southern part of Judah. Here many men gathered around him.

David protected the farmers and shepherds from raids by the Philistines and other tribes. In this way he obtained food and clothing.

When Saul heard that David was hiding in the wilderness of Ziph he picked 3000 soldiers to hunt David.

David's spies told him immediately of the coming of Saul. David approached Saul from the top of the mountain.

Below him in the valley Saul had pitched his camp. Saul lay asleep in the center of the camp. Around him were a few men arranged in a circle. Next came a larger circle of men.

Saul was thus protected by many circles of men.

David, turning to his soldiers, asked, "Who will go down with me to Saul's camp?"

"I will go down with you," answered Abishai, the cousin of David.

Night had descended. David and Abishai approached the camp. A deep slumber had fallen on all of Saul's soldiers. Even the sentries slept.

David and Abishai passed through the outer circle, then through the inner circles of men.

They stood next to the sleeping king. Near him slept the general of his armies, Abner. Saul's spear was stuck in the ground.

Then said Abishai to David, "God has delivered your enemy into your hand this day. Let me smite him once with his own spear, and with one stroke I will destroy your enemy."

And David replied, "Destroy him not. Who can put forth his hand against the Lord's anointed?"

Instead of slaying Saul, they took the spear and the

pitcher of water that were near him. Then quickly they escaped. None knew they had been there. All slept.

David and Abishai climbed to the top of the mountain.

Then David cried out in a loud voice, "Abner awake! Abner awake!"

"Who calls my name?" replied Abner, waking from his deep slumber.

"Why did you not watch over your king? We could have killed King Saul if we wished. You deserve to die!"

Abner recognized David's voice.

David continued, "Where are the king's spear and pitcher? The king was at our mercy, but we would not harm God's anointed."

By now Saul, too, had awakened. Seeing that the pitcher and spear were missing, Saul and Abner realized that David had indeed been in their camp.

Suddenly all of Saul's hatred for David melted away.

"Is this your voice, my son David?" asked Saul with tears in his eyes.

"Yes, my lord," replied David. "Why do you pursue after me? How have I harmed you?"

"I have sinned," said Saul. "Return, my son David. I promise I shall not harm you, because my life was precious in your eyes this day. I know that you could have killed me, but you showed mercy toward me."

"Here is your spear," added David. "Send one of your soldiers and I shall give it to him."

"Blessings on you, David," called out Saul. "May God be with you!"

After the spear had been restored, David and Abishai went back to their camp.

Saul returned to his court. After this incident he never again pursued David.

4. "HOW ARE THE MIGHTY FALLEN!"

Samuel now died, mourned by all Israel. This great leader had united the twelve tribes. He had judged them wisely, and had taught them to obey the laws of Moses. It was Samuel who had chosen Saul to be king, and who had anointed David to succeed Saul.

David was afraid that Saul would change his mind again. How long could **he** hide from Saul if he remained in Israel?

Once more David sought refuge in the land of the Philistines. Knowing how the lords of Gath had almost killed him the first time, David asked for permission to live in the distant village of Ziklag.

The king of Gath gave David permission to live there, and David was safe from Saul at last.

Again war broke out between Saul and the Philistines! David and his 600 men were ordered by the king to join the Philistine army. What was David to do? He could never fight against Israel; yet, if he disobeyed, the Philistines could destroy him.

David's men joined the ranks of the Philistines. David hoped that in the thick of the battle he might help Israel in some way. When the Philistine soldiers recognized David, however, they protested to the king.

"Is not this David of whom it was said that he has killed tens of thousands of Philistines?" The king of the Philistines ordered David to return to Ziklag.

When David arrived in Ziklag he discovered that the Amalekites had burnt the entire city to the ground. The women and children had been taken captive.

Quickly David pursued after the raiders. He overtook them, and defeated them. None of the captives had been harmed.

It was a sad day, however, for Saul and for Israel. Without David as their leader, Israel could not defeat the Philistine army.

The Philistine chariots of iron mowed down the Israelite soldiers. The archers followed behind the chariots, shooting those who had remained alive.

Brave Jonathan fell on the slopes of Mount Gilboa. Near him lay the dead bodies of two of his brothers, and hundreds of Israelites.

At that moment the archers recognized King Saul.

"Death to the king!" they shouted, surrounding him on all sides.

Seeing that escape was impossible Saul turned to his armor-bearer.

"Thrust me through with your sword," he pleaded, "before the Philistines slay me."

The armor-bearer, however, was afraid to touch the king. Saul fell on his own sword. A passing soldier seeing him in great pain thrust him through again so that Saul died.

To mock Israel, the Philistines hung the bodies of Saul and Jonathan on the wall of a nearby city, Beth-Shan.

The men of Jabesh, the city which Saul had once saved, secretly marched at night to Beth-Shan. They recovered the bodies of Saul and Jonathan and gave them decent burial.

When David heard the sad news he wept for Saul and Jonathan. These were his words:

> "How are the mighty fallen!
> I am distressed for you, my brother Jonathan;
> Very pleasant have you been to me,
> Wonderful was your love to me!
> How are the mighty fallen!"

EXERCISES

I. Who? (Review sections 1 and 2, pages 120 to 125.)
1. Who became David's loyal friend?
2. Who sang:

> "Saul has slain his thousands,
> And David his ten thousands"?

3. Who hurled a spear at David?
4. Who fled to Samuel?
5. Who was angry because David did not attend the feast of the new month?
6. Who collected the arrows that had been shot by Jonathan?
7. Who warned David that he must flee?

II. Choose the correct name or word. (Review section 3, pages 125 to 128.)

1. David fled to ————. (Gath, Gilgal)
2. ———— went with David to Saul's camp. (Abishai, Jonathan)
3. Abishai wanted to kill ————. (Abner, Saul)
4. David took Saul's ————. (crown, spear)
5. ———— said, "I have sinned."

III. True or false? (Review section 4, pages 128 to 130.)

1. Samuel had united the 12 tribes.
2. David was sure that Saul would never pursue after him again.
3. David fought against Saul on the side of the Philistines.
4. David defeated the Amalekites who had burnt Ziklag.
5. Saul and Jonathan fell on the field of battle.

IV. Questions for discussion:

1. Do you think that Saul should be called "a hero of Israel"?
2. How did Jonathan prove that he was David's loyal and unselfish friend? Do you know any other stories about very loyal friends?

THINGS TO DO

1. *An Original Story*—Write a story about two friends who were as loyal to each other as David and Jonathan.

2. *New Month*—We see from this chapter that there was an important celebration in honor of the new month.

The new month is still ushered in with special prayers. Find the prayer for the new month in the *Siddur*.

Find out when the next Jewish month begins. Look for the new moon. (The new moon looks like a curved sickle.)

The full moon appears on the 15th day of the month. The following holidays are celebrated at the time of the full moon: Passover, Sukkot, Purim, Tu Bishvat (Israel Arbor Day). Look for the full moon in the heavens when the next one of these holidays is celebrated.

A HISTORY GAME

One student goes out of the room. The other students choose the name of a person or place important in Jewish history. The pupil who is "it" then asks 5 questions. The answers must be either "yes" or "no." The student must guess which name the class has chosen.

King David and King Solomon

CHAPTER XII

DAVID—KING OF ISRAEL

1. THE NEW KING

A S SOON AS Saul had died the tribe of Judah sent messengers to David to come to the city of Hebron.

"You will be our king," they said.

David was crowned king of Judah in Hebron, the city in which Abraham had lived. His first act was to reward the city of Jabesh for recovering the bodies of Saul and Jonathan.

Abner, the general of Saul's army, fled over the Jordan River after the defeat at the hands of the Philistines. Here he crowned Saul's son, Ish-bosheth, king of Israel.

At first there was war between David and Saul's son. David, however, became stronger and stronger while Saul's son became weaker and weaker.

It was well known by now that Samuel had anointed David as king.

"Why do we allow bloodshed?" asked many of the people of Israel. "Did not Samuel anoint David as our king?"

At last, after seven years, Abner decided to support David as king of all Israel.

Meanwhile, two servants of Ish-bosheth, hoping to receive a reward from David, put Ish-bosheth to death.

David was horrified by this crime. Instead of rewarding the servants, he punished them.

All Israel came to Hebron to crown David king.

"Long live King David!" shouted the people. "Long live King David!"

For three days the people rejoiced that at last their great hero reigned as king over a united nation.

David never forgot his loyal friend, Jonathan. After some time had passed David asked, "Is there yet any that is left of the house of Saul that I may show him kindness for Jonathan's sake?"

A servant of Saul's was found and was brought before David.

"Is there anybody left of the house of Saul," asked David, "that I may show the kindness of God unto him?"

And the servant replied, "The son of Jonathan is still alive. His name is Mephi-bosheth. On the day when Israel was defeated by the Philistines, he was a lad of five. His nurse picked him up and fled with him out of fear of the Philistines. The lad fell from his nurse's arms and was badly hurt. Today, he is lame on both feet."

"Call Mephi-bosheth to me," ordered David.

When Jonathan's son appeared before David, he bowed low to the ground.

"Behold your servant," he said.

"Rise," commanded David. "Fear not. I shall surely show you kindness for Jonathan, your father's sake. I hereby restore to you all the land that belonged to Saul. And you will eat at the king's table as a prince."

Jonathan's son thanked David for his great kindness. And all Israel heard and was pleased.

2. THE CAPTURE OF JERUSALEM AND OTHER VICTORIES

David then called Joab, the general of his army, to him. Joab was David's cousin and was made general because of his bravery and his loyalty.

"Hebron is too far in the south to be the capital city," said David.

"Let us pick a strong city as our capital," said Joab.

"I have set my heart on Jerusalem," added David. "Although Joshua defeated the king of Jerusalem, the city itself has never been taken by the Israelites. If we allow Jerusalem to remain in Canaanite hands it will always be a threat to us. We cannot permit such a strong city to divide the northern tribes from the southern tribes."

"Jerusalem will be the most precious jewel in your crown," said Joab. "Our soldiers are ready."

The king of Jerusalem mocked David and Joab when they demanded the surrender of Jerusalem. On the walls of Jerusalem, the king placed lame and blind soldiers.

"The lame and the blind can protect this city," was the reply of the Canaanite king to David.

After brave fighting Joab and his soldiers captured

the city of Jerusalem. They entered by means of a secret tunnel. Last to fall was the fortress on Mount Zion, one of the highest of Jerusalem's mountains.

"Mount Zion will be my dwelling-place," said David.

Jerusalem was now a Hebrew city and capital of Israel. David and his descendants were to make of Jerusalem one of the world's greatest cities.

Jerusalem was at the junction of important roads. One road led from the Jordan River to the Mediterranean coast. Another road led from the south to Damascus and the cities of the north. Standing more than 2000 feet above sea-level, Jerusalem was a great stronghold.

The Philistines then said, "Let us destroy this king before he becomes too strong."

The Philistines gathered a great army. But a new day had dawned for Israel. No longer would Israelites be the slaves of the Philistines.

Marching quickly through mountain passes, David's army surprised the Philistines from the rear.

The Philistines called on their allies for help. But no army could stand before David and his soldiers.

The Philistines suffered one smashing defeat after another at the hands of the Israelites. For almost one hundred years there had been a life and death struggle between the Israelites and the Philistines. But now the struggle was decided in favor of Israel.

David had completed the work of Samson, Eli, Samuel and Saul. The battle against the Philistines was won for all time!

North and south, east and west, David sent his victorious armies. His great empire stretched from the Mediterranean Sea to the Euphrates River, where Abraham had been born.

At last David rested from his wars.

3. "THE LORD IS MY SHEPHERD"

David picked up his harp again and sang as he played. He sang songs of thanksgiving to God for having given Israel victory over its enemies.

David sang of his youth and of his days as a shepherd. He remembered how he used to take care of the sheep.

During the day he would lead the sheep to green fields. There the sheep would pasture, and obtain relief from the hot sun. Toward evening he would find a still pool from which the sheep would drink and satisfy their thirst.

How often the sheep were in danger! As they climbed over the mountains, the shepherd led them in a straight path. One misstep and the sheep might fall over the cliff to his death.

The shepherd tapped with his staff to guide the sheep. No wild animal could approach out of fear of the shepherd's staff.

If a sheep fell and was bruised, the oil in the horn slung over the shepherd's chest, would soothe the bruise.

"I am like the sheep and God is like the shepherd," thought David. "God has guided me and helped me in the face of danger."

And David sang:

> The Lord is my shepherd; I shall not want.
> He maketh me to lie down in green pastures;
> He leadeth me beside the still waters.
> He restoreth my soul;
> He guideth me in straight paths for His name's sake.
>
> Yea, though I walk through the valley of the shadow
>   of death,
> I will fear no evil,
> For Thou art with me;
> Thy rod and Thy staff, they comfort me.
>
> Thou preparest a table before me in the presence of
>   mine enemies;
> Thou hast anointed my head with oil; my cup
>   runneth over.
>
> Surely goodness and mercy shall follow me all the
>   days of my life;
> And I shall dwell in the house of the Lord for ever.

And all Israel loved David's song. The song was later put together with other beautiful songs in praise of God in a book called "The Book of Psalms."

Many, many years later the song was translated from Hebrew into other languages. The song was called "The 23rd Psalm," and became the world's most beloved song.

When the Pilgrims came to Massachusetts Bay, "The Book of Psalms" was one of their most treasured possessions.

"Let us translate the beautiful Hebrew words into our own language," said the Pilgrims.

The Pilgrims poured out their feelings of thanksgiving unto God by translating the 23rd Psalm and the other psalms into their own words. This was the first book ever printed in America and was called "The Bay Psalm Book."

David's song had found its way into the hearts of the builders of a new world!

EXERCISES

I. What is my name? (Review section 1, pages 135 to 137.)

1. I was the first king of Israel. I died in battle while fighting against the Philistines.

2. I was king of Judah in Hebron. After seven years I was crowned king of all Israel.

3. I was the general of Saul's army. After his death I helped his son become king.

4. I was the son of Saul. I succeeded him as king of Israel.

5. I was David's true friend. I was killed in battle with the Philistines.

6. I was the son of Jonathan. King David treated me kindly for my father's sake.

II. Match. (Review section 2, pages 137 to 139.)

Column A	Column B
David	1. Capital of Israel
Hebron	2. Second king of Israel
Jerusalem	3. Mountain in Jerusalem
Joab	4. City where David was crowned king
Philistines	5. General of David's army
Zion	6. Enemy of Israel

III. Answer each question in a complete sentence. (Review section 3, pages 139 to 141.)
1. What work did David do when he was a youth?
2. Whom does David compare to a shepherd?
3. Why does the shepherd carry a staff?
4. In which language did David write the 23rd Psalm?
5. Which was the first book printed in America?

IV. Questions for discussion:
1. In your opinion which was David's greatest achievement?
2. How does a good shepherd help his sheep?

THINGS TO DO

1. *Memory Gem*—Memorize the 23rd Psalm.

2. *Shepherd Life*—Find pictures of shepherds and their sheep in magazines. Explain each picture to the class.

(If the magazine is your own property, clip the picture and paste it in your scrap-book.)

3. *Psalms*—Learn to sing some of the Psalms in English or in Hebrew. Here are some suggestions:

a. "The Lord is My Shepherd"
b. *Hin-neh Mah Tov*
c. *Mizmor L'David* (Psalm 29)
d. *Shir Ha-Maalot* (Psalm 126)

4. *Choral Reading*—Divide the class into groups. Each group reads the lines assigned to it. The lines of the 23rd Psalm might be divided as follows:

Line 1—Solo	Line 4—Solo
Line 2—Boys	Line 5—Boys
Line 3—Girls	Lines 6-8—Solo

Line 9—Girls
Line 10—Boys
Line 11—Girls

Line 12—Solo
Line 13—All

A NUMBER PUZZLE

Take the number of soldiers who fought with Gideon. Add the number of tribes of Israel. Add the number of letters in the name of David's best friend. Divide by the number of commandments on the tablets of stone. Subtract the number of Naomi's sons. The result is David's age when he began to reign in Hebron.

CHAPTER XIII

DAVID
AND THE PROPHET NATHAN

I. THE ARK AND THE TEMPLE

D AVID knew that Samuel had anointed him to be king not to be great in war, but to lead the people to worship one God.

In all things David would ask the advice of Nathan the prophet. After Samuel's death it was Nathan who taught Israel the word of God.

After the capture of Jerusalem, David decided to bring up the ark of God to the capital. For twenty years the ark had been taken care of by a family of Levites in a small village.

With great rejoicing the children of Israel took the ark and brought it to Jerusalem. The *shofar* was blown, and David leaped and danced joyously before the Lord.

As the ark was brought through the gates of Jerusalem David sang:

"Lift up your heads, O you gates,
And be you lifted up, you everlasting doors,

That the King of glory may come in.
Who then is the King of glory?
The Lord of hosts,
He is the King of glory."

A large tent had been pitched on Mount Zion and here the ark rested.

As David looked out from his beautiful palace and saw the tent of the ark, he thought, "It is not right for me to live in such a splendid house while the ark rests in a tent."

David called Nathan the prophet and said, "See now, I dwell in a house of cedar, but the ark of God dwells within curtains. Let me send to Hiram, king of Tyre, for cedars of the Lebanon forest. And I shall build a Temple for the ark."

And Nathan replied, "Go, do all that is in your heart for the Lord is with you."

That night the word of the Lord came unto Nathan saying, "In all the years that I have been with Israel since the days of Moses I have not ordered the children of Israel to build me a house of cedar. David is a man of war and has shed blood. The son of David who will reign after him will be a man of peace. He will build a Temple."

Nathan quickly went to David and told him the words of God. "Because you have been righteous," added Nathan, "the house of David will always reign in Jerusalem."

David lifted his voice in prayer and thanked God that his descendants would reign in Jerusalem.

2. DAVID AND BATHSHEBA

David was separated from his wife, Michal, for several years after she had helped him escape from Saul. When Saul died, Michal was able to rejoin her husband. As was the custom for kings in ancient days, David married many wives.

One day, as David walked on the roof of his palace, he saw a beautiful woman with whom he fell deeply in love.

"Never have I seen a more beautiful woman," he thought.

David sent messengers to inquire about the woman.

Returning to the king the servants reported, "The woman's name is Bathsheba. She is married to one of your soldiers, a man named Uriah."

The king was greatly troubled. How could he wrong one of his own soldiers?

A terrible thought then came to the king. What if the soldier was killed in battle? The king would not be guilty of shedding his blood, but he would be free to marry Bathsheba.

Joab and the army were then besieging a city in the land east of the Jordan.

David wrote a letter to Joab saying, "Put Uriah in the front lines in the thick of the battle."

Several days later enemy soldiers marched out through the gate of the city and attacked the Israelites. Joab and his soldiers fought hard and defeated the enemy.

"Pursue after the enemy as far as the wall of the city," commanded Joab.

From the wall of the city the archers shot at the attacking Israelites, killing several soldiers. Brave Uriah, who had been placed in the front lines, was among those who fell.

Joab chose a messenger to bring news of the battle to the king.

"The king may get angry," warned Joab, "because we came too near to the city wall. If he does get angry then tell him that Uriah was among those who died."

The messenger ran until he arrived, almost breathless, before David.

"What news?" asked David anxiously.

The messenger gave his report and then quickly added, "Uriah was among those killed."

"Tell Joab that I have complete confidence in him," said David. "Despite these losses I am sure that he will soon conquer the city."

In a few days the city fell before Joab.

Bathsheba mourned for Uriah. Then the king sent for her, and Bathsheba was married to David.

The word of God came to Nathan the prophet saying, "David has sinned a great sin. Go to David and tell him the word of the Lord."

3. PROPHET AND KING

"I come to you seeking justice," said Nathan.

"What is wrong?" asked King David.

"There are two men who live in your kingdom in the same city. One is very rich, and the other is very poor. The rich man has servants and flocks and silver and gold.

"The poor man had nothing but one little ewe lamb. The lamb grew up together with him and with his children. It ate at its owner's table and drank of his cup. It was his one prized, beloved possession.

"There came a visitor unto the rich man. And the rich man said to his servant, 'Let us prepare a festive meal in honor of our guest. Slaughter a lamb and serve it before him.'

"As the servant prepared to go to the rich man's flock, his master whispered, 'Do not take one of our lambs. Take the lamb belonging to the poor man.'

"The servant went to the poor man's house, and took the lamb, the poor man's one prized, beloved possession. He killed the lamb and served it to the guest as food.

"What shall be done," asked Nathan, "to the man who has stolen his neighbor's one beloved ewe lamb?"

"Who is this man—he deserves to die!" said David in great anger.

The prophet pointed a long, bony finger at the king and thundered, "You are the man!"

David bowed his head in silence.

"You are the man!" repeated the prophet. "You have everything—a kingdom, wives, servants, riches. And you took the one beloved ewe lamb belonging to one of your own soldiers. You sent Uriah to his death, so that you might marry Bathsheba!"

"I have sinned," said David sadly. "My love for Bath-sheba was so strong that I hardly knew what I was doing. I have committed a great sin."

"Did not God take you from behind the sheep to rule wisely and justly?" demanded Nathan.

"Maybe God will pardon my great sin," replied David meekly. "I shall pray for forgiveness."

"I shall pray for you," said Nathan, "because you have repented."

Once more the prophet had shown that he was more powerful than the king. Mighty David with one word could have ordered his servants to put Nathan to death.

But David knew that the prophet spoke in the name of God. Unless the king ruled with justice he did not deserve to be king.

Nathan had proved that the king was not master. God was master, and the king had to obey the rules of truth and of justice.

EXERCISES

I. Complete each sentence with the correct name or word. (Review section 1, pages 144 to 145.)

    1. David was anointed king by _____. (Nathan, Samuel)

    2. David brought the ark to _____. (Jerusalem, Shiloh)

    3. The ark rested in a _____. (Temple, tent)

    4. Nathan said that a Temple would be built by David's _____. (friend, son)

5. God wanted the Temple to be built by a man of
_____. (peace, war)

II. Arrange the following sentences in the proper order.
(Review section 2, pages 146 to 147.)
   1. Nathan was told to rebuke David.
   2. The enemy marched out through the wall.
   3. Uriah fell in battle.
   4. David fell in love with Bathsheba.
   5. David wrote to Joab to put Uriah in the thick of
      the battle.
   6. David married Bathsheba.

III. Which is right—"rich man" or "poor man"? (Review
      section 3, pages 147 to 149.)
   1. The beloved ewe lamb belonged to the _____.
   2. A visitor came to the house of the _____.
   3. The servant killed the lamb belonging to the
      _____.
   4. Uriah resembled the _____ in the story.
   5. David resembled the _____ in the story.

IV. Questions for discussion:
   1. Nathan said that the Temple must be built by a man
      of peace. In what ways can the synagogue or reli-
      gious school help promote peace?
   2. In which ways did Nathan influence David?
   3. Compare Samuel and Nathan.

THINGS TO DO

1. *Prayer for Peace*—Find a prayer for peace in the prayer
book. Read it to the class.
2. *Film-strip*—Arrange for the showing of a film-strip or
moving picture about the life of King David.

"WHAT'S MY NAME?"—A GAME

Play the game, "What's My Name?" One student is picked as leader. A second pupil then briefly describes a person or a place in the Bible. If the leader guesses the name he remains up, if not the second pupil takes his place. The first one to score five right is the winner.

CHAPTER XIV

"MY SON, ABSALOM!"

1. PRINCE ABSALOM

DAVID'S favorite son was named Absalom. Absalom, however, killed his half-brother, Amnon, in a quarrel.

Out of fear of his father's anger, Absalom fled from David's kingdom.

David mourned for his son, Amnon, but also longed for his exiled son, Absalom. For three years Absalom remained in exile.

Knowing how much King David loved his son, Joab hit on a clever scheme to persuade the king to recall Absalom. He went to a woman in the village of Tekoa who was famous for her wisdom.

"Go to the king, I pray you," said Joab. "Go dressed in the clothes of a mourner who weeps for the loss of a beloved one. And speak the words that I shall put into your mouth."

The wise woman of Tekoa consented to do what Joab requested. She came before King David seeking justice.

152

"Help, O mighty king," she begged, bowing low before David.

"Rise", said the king. "What ails you?"

"I am a widow," replied the wise woman. "I had two sons. They quarreled in the field, and one slew the other. My relatives now demand that the one son who is left be put to death for his misdeed. Thus I shall be left without any children."

"I swear by God," said David, "that not one hair of your son's will fall to the earth. Go to your house, and I shall give orders that your son is not to be harmed."

And the woman said, "O my lord, may I add a few more words?"

"Speak on," replied the king.

"You have spared my son," said the wise woman. "Why then do you not spare your own son, Absalom, who has been sent into exile?"

"Has Joab ordered you to do this?" asked David.

"I see you are wise in all things," replied the woman.

David thanked the wise woman.

He then sent for Joab and said, "I have granted your request. Bring back Absalom to Jerusalem. But he may not see my face."

Joab brought back Absalom to Jerusalem. But for two years David refused to see his son.

"Why has the king allowed me to return?" pleaded Absalom with Joab. "If I cannot see him, would it not have been better for me to remain in exile?"

Joab repeated these words to David. At last, after five

long years, David forgave Absalom. The prince came to
the palace and David kissed his beloved son.

2. THE REBELLION

Absalom said to himself, "I shall now win the hearts
of the people."

Absalom inquired of each man who came to Jerusalem,
"What is your request?"

"I come seeking justice," the Israelite would reply.

To all who were dissatisfied Absalom would say, "Alas,
my father is too old to judge his people. If I were judge
each man would receive justice."

Absalom would thus show friendship to all. In this
manner he stole the hearts of the men of Israel.

One day Absalom requested permission to visit his
birthplace in Hebron to offer thanksgiving unto God.

"Go in peace," said King David.

Absalom sent spies throughout Israel saying, "As soon
as you hear the sound of the *shofar* proclaim Absalom
king."

Absalom was joined in Hebron by Ahithophel, David's
wisest counselor, who supported Absalom.

At the given signal the *shofar* was sounded and the
people shouted, "Long live King Absalom! Long live
King Absalom!"

When David heard the sad news he turned to Joab
and said, "Let us flee before it is too late."

The royal family and the king's body-guard left Jerusalem by way of the Mount of Olives. The people wept
as they saw the king flee.

Among those who fled with David was Hushai, one of his wisest counselors.

"Return to Jerusalem," advised David. "Tell Absalom that you are willing to serve him faithfully as you have served me all these years. Try to defeat the advice of Ahithophel, for he is a wise man and can do us much harm."

Hushai returned just as Absalom entered Jerusalem.

"Long live King Absalom!" said Hushai bowing low. "I wish to serve the man whom God and the people have chosen as king."

The prince was happy that he was supported by so many wise men.

Absalom then turned to Ahithophel for advice.

"What shall we do now?" he asked.

"Let me choose 12,000 men," replied Ahithophel. "I shall pursue after David while he is still weary. We shall slay David only. There will be no need to battle with his army for they are not yet ready for war."

The advice pleased Absalom.

Then said Absalom, "Call Hushai also, and let us hear what he says."

When Hushai was told of Ahithophel's advice he said, "The counsel given to you by Ahithophel is not good. You know that David is a mighty man of war. His soldiers are enraged and will fight like a bear robbed of its cubs. David is surely in hiding and will not easily be found. If some of your soldiers are killed in battle, the men of Israel will lose heart and will desert you."

"What then must be done?" asked Absalom.

"Let all Israel be gathered together from Dan unto Beersheba. When they hear that David has fled they will rally to your support. Then we can fight against David and Joab and defeat them, for we shall be many and they will be few."

Absalom was greatly pleased by Hushai's advice.

"Let us wait in Jerusalem," said Absalom, "until we have gathered a large army. Then we can easily defeat David. The advice of Hushai is better than the advice of Ahithophel."

When Ahithophel saw that his advice was not followed, he arose, saddled his donkey and rode to his own city. There he strangled himself.

Hushai quickly sent spies to David with the news. David and Joab rejoiced, for had they been attacked immediately they were too weak and weary to resist.

They crossed the Jordan at Gilgal and had time to form a new army east of the Jordan.

Hushai's advice had saved David's life.

3. THE DEATH OF ABSALOM

The Israelites east of the Jordan rallied to David's aid. They brought sheep, wheat, barley, cheese and fruits to feed his soldiers.

Absalom and his army crossed the Jordan to do battle with David.

David prepared to lead the army, but the soldiers would not let him go forth to the battle.

"If you are captured then we are all lost," said Joab and his men.

David consented to remain at the city-gate to await news of the battle.

The king called Joab and his captains and warned them, "Deal gently for my sake with Absalom."

Just as David had forgiven Saul, so too he forgave Absalom, his beloved son.

"Perhaps the young man is not at fault," thought David. "Maybe this is punishment for my sin."

It was a far-flung battle that spread throughout the country on both sides of the Jordan.

Absalom's men were badly defeated by Joab, his brother Abishai and their many brave soldiers.

Absalom was the victim of a strange accident. As he rode on a mule through the forest, his long hair caught in the thick bough of an oak tree.

The mule ran ahead leaving Absalom suspended by his hair from the tree.

One of the soldiers passing by recognized Absalom and ran to report the news to Joab.

"Why didn't you kill him?" demanded Joab. "I would have given you ten pieces of silver as a reward."

"I would not have done it for a thousand pieces of silver," said the soldier. "I heard the king warn the soldiers not to harm Absalom."

Joab and ten men ran to the tree from which Absalom was suspended. The soldiers quickly slew the prince, Joab throwing the first three darts.

A negro soldier in David's army was sent as a messenger to bring news of the victory to the king.

David waited anxiously at the city gate.

"Is all well?" asked David as the messenger arrived.

"Good tidings!" replied the messenger. "God has given you victory over your enemies."

"And Absalom—is he well?" asked David eagerly.

"Absalom is dead," said the messenger.

The king was greatly moved, and could not restrain his tears.

"O my son, Absalom! My son, my son Absalom!" wept the king. "Would I had died for you, O Absalom, my son, my son!"

And Joab was told, "Behold, the king is weeping for Absalom."

The victory that day was turned into mourning. The soldiers entered the city as if they were deserters running away from battle.

And David cried in a loud voice, "O my son, Absalom! O Absalom, my son, my son!"

Joab angrily went to the king and said, "If you continue to mourn for Absalom, none will remain with you. Did not the soldiers risk their lives to save you and your family? Go forth to speak to the people, and thank them for winning this great victory."

David dried his tears and went out to greet his brave soldiers.

And all Israel heard that David's army had defeated the rebels, and Israel rejoiced.

EXERCISES

I. Who said to whom? (Review section 1, pages 152 to 154.)

1. "Go to the king, I pray you. Go dressed in the clothes of a mourner who weeps for the loss of a beloved one."
2. "My relatives now demand that the one son who is left be put to death for his misdeed."
3. "I shall give orders that your son is not to be harmed."
4. "Bring back Absalom to Jerusalem."
5. "If I cannot see him, would it not have been better for me to remain in exile?"

II. Complete each sentence. (Review section 2, pages 154 to 156.)

ABSALOM, AHITHOPHEL, DAVID, HEBRON, HUSHAI

1. _____ said that his father did not rule justly.
2. Absalom's rebellion began in the city of _____.
3. _____ fled from Jerusalem.
4. _____ advised that Absalom pursue after David immediately.
5. _____ advised that Absalom wait until he had gathered a larger army.

III. True or false? (Review section 3, pages 156 to 158.)

1. Absalom crossed the Jordan to fight against David.
2. David's soldiers wanted the king to lead them into battle in person.
3. David's army was defeated by Absalom.
4. Absalom was caught by his hair in the bough of a tree.
5. David mourned for his son, "O my son, Absalom!"

IV. Questions for discussion:
1. Compare Absalom and Abimelech, the son of Gideon.
2. Was Joab right in ordering Absalom's death?
3. David has been called "shepherd, warrior, musician, poet, statesman, king, judge." Explain.

THINGS TO DO

1. *Legends About David*—Since David was Israel's greatest king, many legends have grown up about him. Read a legend about David, and tell the story to the class. *The Legends of the Jews*, Volume IV, by Louis Ginzberg contains many interesting legends. The story of the honey jars is found on page 85; the story of Saul's pursuit is on page 89; Joab's adventures are told on page 97; the story of David's tomb is on page 119.

Many of the David legends are found in a book by the great poet, Bialik, called *And It Came To Pass*. They may also be read in Hyman Goldin's *The Book of Legends*.

2. *Israeli Stamps*—Pictures of Jerusalem can be seen on Israeli stamps. One of the scenes is the Tower of David.

Write to the Israeli consul and inquire about the purchase of Israeli stamps. Make a special collection of these stamps. Find out what each picture represents.

A PUZZLE

Write the name of David's best friend. Take away the letters in the name of the prophet who advised David. Add the name of the first Hebrew. Substract the name of the animal from which the *shofar* is obtained. Subtract the first two letters of the name of Ishmael's mother.

The result is the name of a brave soldier in David's army.

CHAPTER XV

AN UNDERSTANDING HEART

1. THE LAST DAYS OF KING DAVID

DAVID reigned as king for forty years. In Hebron he reigned for seven years, and in Jerusalem for 33 years.

David became ill at the age of 70. Knowing that he did not have much longer to live, he called Bathsheba and promised that their son Solomon would succeed him as king.

Solomon had an older brother named Adonijah. It was his ambition to become king, and he was supported by Joab and other important officers.

One day Adonijah invited all of the king's sons, except Solomon, and many of the king's servants to a sacrifice. There the people shouted, "Long live King Adonijah! Long live King Adonijah!"

As soon as Nathan the prophet heard what was happening he warned Bathsheba that Solomon's life was in danger.

"Go to the king and remind him of his oath that Solomon would reign after him. If not, Adonijah will become

king, and he will put Solomon to death as a dangerous rival.
I shall try to help you."

Bathsheba hurried to the king's chamber.

"What is your wish, Bathsheba?" asked David.

"You once swore," replied Bathsheba, "that Solomon
would succeed you as king. Today, without your knowing
it, Adonijah has prepared a feast, and the people shout that
he is king. Unless you declare Solomon as king our lives
will be in danger."

While she spoke to David a servant announced that
Nathan wished to see David.

The prophet bowed low before the king and asked, "O
lord, is it with your consent that Adonijah has declared
himself king? If not, do not delay but choose your succes-
sor today."

David replied, "Call my servants, and I shall proclaim
Solomon as the new king."

When David's chief officers had gathered in his cham-
ber he said, "Let my son Solomon ride on the royal mule.
Clothe him in the king's garments. Take him to the foun-
tain of Gihon where the people gather to draw water. Let
Nathan anoint him with oil and proclaim him king over
Judah and Israel."

Nathan and the officers carried out the king's command.
As soon as Solomon was anointed with oil, the people
shouted, "Long live King Solomon! Long live King
Solomon!"

The musicians played on the pipes, and the people rejoiced with singing and with shouts of joy.

Solomon was then led to the palace and placed on David's throne.

As soon as Adonijah and Joab heard what had been done, they ended their feast for they knew that their plans had been defeated.

David then commanded Solomon, "Be strong, and obey the Lord, your God. Keep his commandments according to that which is written in the law of Moses. For if you walk in His ways, God will bless you and the people of Israel."

When David died he was greatly mourned by Judah and Israel. David was buried on Mount Zion where his tomb remains to this very day.

David was the greatest king the Hebrew people ever had. There are many reasons why the people never forgot the shepherd lad who became a great king:

1. He defeated the giant, Goliath.

2. He smashed the power of the Philistines so that they never threatened Israel again.

3. He made Jerusalem the capital of Israel.

4. He urged the people to follow the laws of God, and helped make Jerusalem a holy city.

5. He extended the borders of Israel so that it became a large and powerful nation.

6. He kept the nation united by showing kindness to the house of Saul and to other rivals.

7. He ruled wisely and justly and obeyed the words of God as taught by the prophets.

8. He made treaties of peace with many rulers such as Hiram, the king of Tyre.

9. He wrote beautiful psalms which have found their way to the heart of all mankind.

10. He founded the royal family which would rule in Jerusalem for 450 years.

It is no wonder, therefore, that the people dreamed of the day when a descendant of David would rule once again in Jerusalem as the Messiah, or anointed one.

The name David means "beloved"; David was indeed a beloved king.

2. SOLOMON'S DREAM

After Solomon became king he went to the city of Gibeon to offer a sacrifice unto God.

And God appeared to Solomon in a dream by night.

And God said, "Ask for a favor of Me, and I shall grant it."

Solomon replied, "O Lord, You have shown great kindness to David, my father, who served You with a pure heart. I have become king in David's place, and I am but a little child.

"Give me, therefore, I pray, an understanding heart to judge Your people. Teach me to know the difference between good and evil. For who can judge such a large nation without Your help?"

Solomon's request pleased the Lord.

And God said, "Because you did not ask for riches, or long life, or power, but for an understanding heart, I shall grant your request. I shall bless you with a wise and under-standing heart to do justice. But also I shall give you the things that you did not ask for—riches, honor, power and long life."

Solomon awoke, and behold it was a dream.

Solomon returned to Jerusalem where he offered a thanksgiving sacrifice before the ark of God. And the king made a great feast for his servants, and for all the people.

Solomon's dream came true. He showed wisdom and kindness in judging the people.

And all Israel praised the wise king who ruled in the place of David, his father.

3. A WISE DECISION

Shortly after his dream Solomon had to make a very difficult decision.

Two women came before the king for judgment.

The first woman said, "Oh, my lord, I and this woman dwell in the same house. I gave birth to a child, and a little while later, my neighbor gave birth to a child.

"One night her child died. She arose, came to my bed, and took the live child from me. The dead child she put in the place of the live child.

"When I arose in the morning I found that the child was dead. But when I looked closely I saw that it was not my child.

"My lord, I demand justice. Give me back my child!"

Solomon turned to the second woman and asked, "What have you to say?"

"This woman lies," replied the second mother. "The live child is mine. Because of grief she has gone out of her mind, and claims my child as her own."

"It is my child who lives," answered the first woman in anger. "The dead child is hers."

"Are there any witnesses to prove what you say?" asked the king.

"There were no others in the house," replied the two women.

"Each one claims the living child is hers, but neither has any proof," thought Solomon. "How can I decide who is the real mother?"

"Bring in the living child," ordered the king.

The child was brought in.

"Fetch me a sword," commanded Solomon. When the sword was brought, the king said, "Divide the living child in two. Give half to each."

"That is fair," said the second woman. "Let it be neither mine nor hers. Divide it."

The real mother, whose heart yearned for the child, turned to the king in tears, "Save the child, my lord! Give it to her but do not slay it!"

Then the king said, "You are the real mother! You have the heart of a mother."

Solomon turned to his servants and commanded, "Give her the living child. Do not slay it. She is the real mother!"

When Israel heard of the king's judgment, the people said, "Solomon has the wisdom of God. He has an understanding heart to do justice and to rule wisely."

EXERCISES

I. Match. (Review section 1, pages 161 to 164.)

Column A	Column B
Adonijah	1. Made Jerusalem capital
Bathsheba	2. Prophet
David	3. Mother of new king
Nathan	4. Third king of Israel
Solomon	5. Brother of king

II. Fill in the correct name or phrase. (Review section 2, pages 164 to 165.)

1. Solomon went to _____ to offer a sacrifice. (Gibeon, Shiloh)
2. God appeared in a dream to _____. (David, Solomon)
3. Solomon asked for _____. (an understanding heart, long life)
4. God promised Solomon _____ than he asked for. (less, more)
5. Solomon returned to _____. (Hebron, Jerusalem)

III. Answer each question in a complete sentence. (Review section 3, pages 165 to 166.)

1. Who came to Solomon for judgment?
2. Why did the second woman take the other woman's child?
3. What did Solomon command?
4. What did the real mother say when she heard the command?
5. Why did Solomon decide that she was the real mother?

IV. Questions for discussion:
1. Compare the achievements of Saul and of David.
2. What other dreams have we read about in the Bible?
3. What is meant by "a wise and understanding heart"? How did Solomon prove that he had an understanding heart?

THINGS TO DO

1. *Story Hour*—Tell the class about a story you have read where a wise decision was made.

2. *Solomon's Temple*—Make a clay or wooden model of Solomon's Temple.

IN JEWISH HISTORY-LAND

Each child says, "I traveled in Jewish History-Land and there I saw _____." The first student mentions the name of a person or place beginning with A; the second student mentions a name beginning with B, etc. The pupil who cannot think of a name is out.

Here are some hints for the difficult letters:

F—City of Four (another name for Hebron)
Q—Queen of Sheba
T—Tel-Aviv
V—Vashti (wife of Persian king in Purim story)
W—Weizmann (first president of new state of Israel)
X—Xerxes (another name for King Ahasuerus in Purim story)
Y—Yemen (land from which Yemenite Jews come)
Z—Zion

CHAPTER XVI

WISE KING SOLOMON

I. BUILDING THE TEMPLE

D AVID had wanted to build a Temple, but was warned not to do so because he was a man of war.

Solomon was blessed with peace. David, his father, had built such a strong nation that there was no need for war. Solomon's name means peace.

As soon as he could, Solomon began to build the Temple.

He sent messengers to David's friend, Hiram, the king of Tyre saying, "I am building a Temple unto God. Let your servants chop down cedar trees in the forest of Lebanon for the Temple. My servants will work alongside of your servants. And I shall send your workers a rich reward."

Hiram replied, "I rejoice that God has blessed Israel with a wise king. My servants will do all that you ask. They will bring the logs of wood to the sea and build them into rafts. Then they will float the rafts to the coast of Israel."

Solomon sent thousands of men to Lebanon to work in the forests. Thousands of others were busy in the mountains around Jerusalem hewing large stones for the foundation of the Temple.

The greatest artists of Israel helped plan the building, and shape the instruments to be used in the Temple.

Many of the instruments were made of copper. Where did Solomon obtain copper? For years this remained a mystery, but in 1952 engineers from the state of Israel found King Solomon's mines about 20 miles north of the Gulf of Akaba.

The copper was refined in Elath, a port at the north of the Gulf of Akaba. The wind blowing from the north was so strong that intense heat could be created by using the proper fuel. In these fires the copper was refined.

The refineries, the largest in ancient times, were recently found. The exact process used by King Solomon, however, is still a mystery.

At one end of the Temple, Solomon built a room called the Holy of Holies. Here the ark of God, containing the ten commandments, was placed.

In the Temple was a golden altar for sacrifices. On each side stood five large candlesticks. Each *menorah*, or candlestick, was made, in part, of gold.

At last, after seven and a half years of labor, the Temple was finished.

2. THE TEMPLE SERVICE

Solomon called the people together to rejoice over the

building of the Temple. For seven days the king and his servants offered sacrifices and prayed unto God.

King Solomon lifted his hands in prayer unto God and said, "O Lord, God of Israel, hear our prayers when we pray unto You. Bless us with peace and with plenty. We will strive with all our hearts to carry out Your laws. Bless, also, the strangers from other lands who will come to this Temple to pray unto You."

After that the people celebrated the holiday of Sukkot. The farmers who had just gathered in their grapes and their fruits came to offer thanksgiving unto God.

For almost 400 years the Temple of Solomon served as a house of worship for the Hebrew nation.

Three times a year the people made a special journey to the Temple. On Passover, after the barley harvest, they came to celebrate the freeing of the Israelites from slavery in Egypt. On Shavuot they came, after the wheat harvest, with their first fruits, and celebrated the granting of the ten commandments. On Sukkot they came, after the grape harvest, to mark the wandering of the Israelites in the desert for forty years.

On Rosh Ha-Shanah, on the Day of Atonement, on Sabbaths and at the beginning of new months special services were held.

Each day of the year there were prayers and sacrifices. The *Kohanim*, or priests, were in charge of the sacrifices. The Levites played on harps and on lyres, with cymbals and with timbrels, and sang the songs of David in praise of God.

The people would join in the beautiful songs of praise:

A Psalm of Thanksgiving

Shout unto the Lord, all the earth.
Serve the Lord with gladness;
Come before His presence with singing.

Know ye that the Lord He is God;
It is He that hath made us, and we are His,
His people, and the flock of His pasture.

Enter into His gates with thanksgiving,
And into His courts with praise;
Give thanks unto Him, and bless His name.

For the Lord is good; His mercy endureth forever;
And His faithfulness unto all generations.

3. THE VISIT OF THE QUEEN OF SHEBA

Solomon built a beautiful palace for himself with the help of Hiram, the king of Tyre. He also built a splendid palace for the daughter of Pharaoh whom he had married.

Jerusalem had now become a great capital. Solomon strengthened the walls of Jerusalem, and built a new wall in some places. He brought thousands of horses from Egypt, and his chariots were seen everywhere.

When the Queen of Sheba heard of Solomon's splendor and of his wisdom, she said to her servants, "Let us go to visit this great king, to see his court with our own eyes."

SOLOMON DEDICATING THE TEMPLE

Bringing with her camels laden with gold and spices, the queen left the land of Sheba and journeyed to Jerusalem.

After hearing Solomon's wise sayings and after seeing his splendor, the Queen of Sheba said, "It was a true report that I heard in my own land of your wisdom. However, I could not believe what I heard until I saw it for myself. Happy are your servants who hear your wisdom each day. Blessed be the Lord your God who made you king to do justice and righteousness."

The Bible tells us that the Queen of Sheba asked Solomon "hard questions." There are many legends about the riddles that Solomon had to answer.

According to the legend, there is one question Solomon would have failed to answer were it not for a bee.

Sleeping in his garden one afternoon, Solomon's nose was stung by a little bee. Solomon, who knew the language of birds and insects, according to the legend, wanted to order his servants to put the bee to death.

"I'm only a baby bee," pleaded the bee for its life. "I thought your nose was a flower. Spare my life and someday I shall help you when you are in trouble."

Solomon, whose nose by this time had swelled to the size of a pumpkin, smiled at the thought that the bee might help him. He took pity on the little bee, however, and pardoned it.

When the Queen of Sheba visited King Solomon, she placed before him real and artificial flowers.

"Which are real and which are artificial?" she asked.

So alike were the flowers in fragrance, color and appearance that it was impossible for Solomon to tell which flowers were real and which were not.

The king was about to admit his failure to answer the question when he heard a familiar buzzing. Looking up he saw his old friend, the bee, at the window.

Solomon raised the window to greet the bee. Immediately the bee flew to the real flowers.

"These are the real ones," said Solomon to the Queen of Sheba.

The bee had kept its promise by helping him at a difficult moment.

The queen of Sheba finally returned to her own land carrying many rare gifts as a present from the great king.

4. TRADE AND THE SPREAD OF THE HEBREW ALPHABET

Much of Solomon's wealth was brought to Israel by his navy. Solomon built ships that sailed alongside of the ships of Hiram, king of Tyre.

The city of Tyre was one of the chief cities of the land of Phoenicia, just north of Israel. The Phoenicians were great sailors. Their ships sailed in the Mediterranean along the coast of Africa. They reached as far as Spain.

Once each three years the ships of Hiram and of Solomon set sail for Tarshish. This is probably an ancient name for Spain. After three years the ships would return bringing precious objects.

Another fleet owned by Solomon and Hiram would set sail from the Gulf of Akaba into the Red Sea and the Indian Ocean to a land called Ophir.

These ships would bring back gold, silver, ivory, spices, sandal-wood, and rare animals such as apes and peacocks.

In return the ships of Solomon and Hiram would sell olive-oil, wine, wheat, honey and a special purple dye. The dye, which only Phoenicians knew how to make, was manufactured from shells found on the shore of the Mediterranean.

The sailors of Phoenicia and Israel brought something even more precious from their homeland to the rest of the world—the alphabet. We are not sure when the other nations borrowed the Hebrew alphabet as the basis of their own. It is very possible that the sailors of Solomon and Hiram were the first to introduce the letters of the Hebrew alphabet to other countries.

Most nations had some form of picture writing. But those who spoke Hebrew used an alphabet where each letter stood for one sound. The alphabet is one of the greatest inventions in the history of mankind.

The Phoenicians and Hebrews spoke almost the same language. There were only a few small differences between the language of Solomon's servants and the language of Hiram's servants.

When the Greeks saw words written in Hebrew they began to borrow the letters of the alphabet. The first letter of the Hebrew alphabet, "aleph," they called "alpha." The second letter of the Hebrew alphabet, "bet", they called "beta," etc. These letters became "a" and "b" in English.

Later the Greeks added a few letters of their own.

The Romans learned the alphabet from the Greeks, and

English-speaking peoples learned the alphabet from the Romans.

It is not hard to recognize the Hebrew letters "aleph" and "bet" in the word "alphabet."

Of course, the Greeks did not begin to use the alphabet right away. It is possible that more than a hundred years passed before they used the letters to which they had been introduced by the sailors of Israel and Phoenicia.

The alphabet, one of mankind's greatest inventions, we owe to the Hebrew language as spoken by the Israelites and Phoenicians.

5. PROVERBS

Because of the use of the alphabet it was easy for Solomon and his wise men to write down the history of Israel. They also wrote poems and wise sayings.

Many of Solomon's wise sayings are found in a book of the Bible called "Proverbs." These sayings are so popular that they have found their way into nearly every language.

When we are lazy, we are told, "Go to the ant, thou sluggard." A lazy person, or sluggard, feels ashamed when he sees how hard at work the ants are. They do not seem to need anybody to stand over them to urge them to work harder.

Here are Solomon's words:

> "Go to the ant, thou sluggard;
> Consider her ways, and be wise;
> Which having no chief,

Overseer, or ruler
Provides her bread in the summer,
And gathers her food in the harvest."

How should one reply to an angry remark? According to Solomon, "A soft answer turneth away wrath" (anger).

Here is one proverb about which people differ. Solomon said, "He that spares his rod hates his son." Do you agree that physical punishment is necessary in bringing up children?

Doctors would agree with Solomon when he says, "A merry heart is a good medicine."

Those who are thoughtless in what they say should remember this proverb, "Death and life are in the power of the tongue."

Solomon believed that education will help us throughout life as shown by this saying:

"Train a child in the way he should go,
    And even when he is old, he will not depart
        from it."

Abraham Lincoln liked the proverb which taught that the man who can conquer his own weaknesses is greater than the soldier who conquers a city:

"He that is slow to anger is better than the
        mighty;
    And he that rules his spirit than he
        that takes a city."

The conceited person should remember the warning, "Be not wise in your own eyes."

The boaster is reminded that "Pride goes before destruction."

Have you ever read of a person who prepared a weapon against his neighbor but who fell by that same weapon? Solomon warns us that wicked people often dig their own graves in the proverb:

> "Who digs a pit shall fall therein;
> And he that rolls a stone, it shall
> return upon him."

The man who works hard need not fear hunger, said Solomon, for "he that tills his ground shall have plenty of bread."

The wise sayings found in the book called "Proverbs" help us lead a good life.

EXERCISES

I. True or false? (Review sections 1 and 2, pages 169 to 172.)
   1. Solomon fought many wars.
   2. Hiram, king of Tyre, chopped down cedar trees in the forest of Lebanon to help Solomon build the Temple.
   3. It took seven months to build the Temple.
   4. The people of Israel made a special journey to the Temple on Passover, on Shavuot, and on Sukkot.

5. The Levites sang Psalms and songs of David in the Temple.

II. Complete each sentence. (Review sections 3 and 4, pages 172 to 177.)

Hebrew, Hiram, Sheba, Solomon, Tarshish

1. _____, king of Tyre, helped Solomon build a palace.

2. A queen came from the land of _____ to visit Solomon because she heard of his great wisdom.

3. There is a legend that a bee helped _____ answer a difficult question.

4. The navies of Hiram and Solomon visited _____ once in three years.

5. The _____ alphabet was the first alphabet.

III. Find a proverb that might help each of the following people. (Review section 5, pages 177 to 179.)

1. A sick person

2. A lazy person

3. A conceited person

4. A person lacking in self-control

5. A person who says foolish things because he speaks without thinking.

IV. Questions for discussion:

1. In which ways was Solomon a great king?

2. Why is the invention of the alphabet so important?

3. Select a proverb by Solomon that you like.

REVIEW QUESTIONS
for Units Three and Four (pages 87 to 180)

1. What were the main achievements of each king of Israel?

2. Tell about the progress made by Israel in the following matters during the reigns of Saul, David and Solomon:

   a. uniting the 12 tribes
   b. fighting against hostile neighbors
   c. worshiping God.

3. The period of Saul, David and Solomon is called the period of the United Kingdom. Why is this one of the great periods in Jewish history?

4. Why is each of the following important in Jewish history?

   Hannah, Eli, Samuel, Nahash the Ammonite, Jonathan, Jesse, Goliath, Michal, Abner, Abishai, Ish-bosheth, Joab, Mephi-bosheth, Nathan, Uriah, Bathsheba, Absalom, Ahithophel, Hushai, Adonijah, Hiram, Queen of Sheba.

5. Explain each of the following phrases:

   a. the ark of God
   b. shibboleth
   c. "Give us a king."
   d. the anointed of God
   e. the shepherd versus the giant
   f. as loyal as David and Jonathan
   g. "Saul has slain his thousands"
   h. "Is Saul, too, among the prophets?"
   i. "How are the mighty fallen!"
   j. "The Lord is my shepherd."
   k. The Bay Psalm Book
   l. a precious, beloved ewe lamb
   m. "My son, Absalom!"
   n. an understanding heart
   o. "Go to the ant, thou sluggard."

TEST

on Units Three and Four

I. What is my name? (30 points)

1. I warned Israel not to select a king.
2. I was *Kohen Gadol* in Shiloh. I died when I heard that the ark of God was captured in battle.
3. I brought my son to Shiloh to serve in the house of God when my prayer was answered.
4. I was a farmer in Bethlehem. One of my sons became king.
5. I was loyal to my friend even though it meant I must give up the throne.
6. I went looking for donkeys and found a kingdom.
7. I supported the son of Saul as king over Israel. I was a general in Saul's army.
8. I helped defeat Absalom by giving advice which he should not have followed.
9. I rebuked David by telling him a story about a precious, beloved ewe lamb.
10. I was king of Tyre. I helped Solomon build the Temple and his palace.

II. Who said to whom? (20 points)

1. "I am a woman of sorrowful spirit for God has not blessed me with any children."
2. "The king will take your sons to drive his chariots. He will force them to plow his ground and to make his weapons."
3. "How can you fight against this Philistine? You are but a youth, and Goliath is a mighty man of war."
4. "If I wave to the lad, 'Go farther', then you will know that the king seeks your life."

5. "Why did you not watch over your king? We could have killed King Saul if we wished."
6. "I shall surely show you kindness for Jonathan, your father's sake."
7. "You took the one beloved ewe lamb belonging to one of your own soldiers."
8. "If you continue to mourn for Absalom, none will remain with you."
9. "Give me an understanding heart to judge Your people."
10. "Let your servants chop down cedar trees in the forest of Lebanon for the Temple."

III. Fill in the name of the king which fits each statement. (24 points)
1. He was the first king of Israel. _____
2. He sent ships to Tarshish. _____
3. He made Jerusalem the capital. _____
4. He defeated the Amalekites but was too lenient with the king. _____
5. He wrote the 23rd Psalm. _____
6. He built the Temple in Jerusalem. _____
7. He smashed the power of the Philistines so that they never threatened Israel again. _____
8. He made a wise decision because he understood the heart of a parent. _____

IV. Answer each question in a complete sentence. (16 points)
1. Why was Samuel angry when the people asked for a king?
2. How did Jonathan prove that he was David's loyal friend?
3. Why did Nathan tell David not to build the Temple?

4. What did Solomon ask for when God appeared to him in a dream at Gibeon?

V. Match. (10 points)

Column A	Column B
"O Absalom, my son!"	1. David weeping for Saul and Jonathan
"Go to the ant, thou sluggard."	2. David weeping for a prince killed by Joab
"How are the mighty fallen!"	3. The 23rd Psalm
"Saul has slain his thousands And David his ten thousands"	4. Proverbs of Solomon
"The Lord is my shepherd."	5. Victory song of women of Israel

UNIT FIVE

The Divided Kingdom

CHAPTER XVII

THE REVOLT OF
THE TEN TRIBES OF ISRAEL

1. SOLOMON'S FAULTS

ALTHOUGH they loved King Solomon, the people had many complaints.

Their first complaint was that Solomon used forced labor. 30,000 men were used to cut down wood in the forests of Lebanon. This labor force was divided into three groups. 10,000 men were sent for a month each to Lebanon.

After a month, the 10,000 would return, and their place would be taken by a second group, etc. After two months at home the first group would again be sent to the Lebanon forest.

80,000 men were in the labor force that cut stone out of the mountains of Israel. Thousands of others carried burdens from the sea or from the mountains to Jerusalem.

A second complaint was that Solomon taxed the people heavily. In order to pay Hiram, the king would gather wheat, barley, fruits and olive oil from the farmers.

If Solomon had built the Temple only, there might have been no complaints. But besides the Temple, Solomon built a palace for himself and palaces for many of his wives. It took thirteen years to build his palace alone.

The people remembered Samuel's warning against selecting a king. He had said that the king would take their sons as soldiers, and their daughters as servants. He would take their fields, and vineyards and sheep.

"We are like slaves," the people complained.

Of course, Israel enjoyed many benefits. If it were not for his standing army, Solomon might not be able to preserve peace. Thanks to his fleet, the standard of living rose. There were many new things that the people could buy because of trade with other nations.

But the people still did not like to give away the fruits of their labor as taxes.

A third complaint was that Solomon had introduced foreign customs. Never before had so many Egyptian horses been seen in the land. Chariots were everywhere. Solomon's wives loved luxury, and worshiped idols.

Out of love for his wives Solomon permitted them to build altars for their gods. Altars were built unto the god of Moab, and the god of Ammon and the god of the Phoenicians.

And the Lord God was angry with Solomon because he had not obeyed His laws. And God sent word to the prophet, "Part of the kingdom will be taken from the house of Solomon. But for David's sake, part of the kingdom will remain."

2. JEROBOAM

One of Solomon's officers was a man named Jeroboam of the tribe of Ephraim. When Solomon repaired the wall around Jerusalem, he noticed the great skill of Jeroboam.

Solomon called Jeroboam to him and said, "Because of your fine work I shall place you in charge of the forced labor for the tribes of Ephraim and Manasseh."

One day as Jeroboam left Jerusalem he met the prophet Ahijah of the city of Shiloh.

"I have a message for you," said Ahijah to Jeroboam.

Jeroboam quietly followed the prophet until they were alone in the field.

"What do you wish to tell me?" asked Jeroboam.

The prophet, who was clad in a new mantle, removed the garment. He ripped the coat into twelve pieces. Ten of the pieces he handed to Jeroboam.

"What is the meaning of this?" asked Jeroboam in amazement.

"Thus will God tear Solomon's kingdom apart," replied the prophet. "Ten parts He will give to you to rule over. Obey His laws and God will make your children and your children's children to reign as kings.

"Ten tribes will follow you, but two tribes, Judah and Benjamin, will remain with Solomon's son.

"This will God do because Solomon has forgotten the laws of God, and has permitted the worship of false gods in Jerusalem.

"But for the sake of David, the servant of God, the kingdom will not be taken away entirely from his children. Nor will this happen in the lifetime of Solomon."

Nothing escaped the sharp notice of Solomon's officers. They had seen the prophet speaking to Jeroboam, and were anxious to find out what he said.

Soon the truth was known. Solomon was afraid to harm the prophet, but he tried to arrest Jeroboam.

Jeroboam, however, was warned in time. He fled to Egypt. Solomon's father-in-law, Pharaoh of Egypt, was no longer alive.

The new Pharaoh welcomed Jeroboam, and gave him refuge at his court.

Jeroboam waited until the death of Solomon before he raised the banner of rebellion.

3. THE REVOLT

Solomon reigned for 40 years. After Solomon's death, his son, Rehoboam, became king in his place.

The children of Israel gathered in Shechem to crown him king. Jeroboam returned from Egypt and came to Shechem to see what would happen.

The Israelites, with Jeroboam at their head, came to the new king and said, "Your father, Solomon, placed a heavy burden upon us. Make our burden lighter, and we shall serve you."

Rehoboam replied, "Return in three days, and I shall give you my answer."

Rehoboam turned to his advisers and asked for their counsel.

The older and wiser men who had served Solomon said, "If you speak kind words to the people, then they will gladly serve you."

Rehoboam then took counsel with the younger men who had grown up with him.

"What reply shall we give to the people who demand that we make their burden lighter?" asked Rehoboam.

"You must show them immediately that you are master," advised his friends. "You must say that your little finger is stronger than your father's whole hand. You must tell them that you will add to their burdens. Warn them that if your father punished them with whips, you will punish them with heavy lashes."

Rehoboam accepted the advice of his younger friends.

When the people returned on the third day Rehoboam said harshly, "How dare you make such impudent demands? I will add to your burden. If my father punished you with whips, I will punish you with heavy lashes."

The people were prepared for such an answer.

"To your tents, O Israel," called out Jeroboam. "What portion have we in the house of David?"

"To your tents, O Israel," shouted the people.

Rehoboam knew that he had made a terrible mistake.

"I should have taken the advice of my father's advisers," said Rehoboam.

Turning to one of the officers, the king said, "Hurry after them. Tell them to return and I shall deal kindly with them."

The officer hurried after the Israelites.

"Come back," shouted the officer. "I have a message from the king for you."

"I know that man," cried an Israelite. "He is in charge of the forced labor. Stone him!"

"Stone him! Stone him!" shouted the people.

The mob turned on the officer and stoned him to death.

"Those stones were aimed at me," thought Rehoboam.

Quickly he entered his chariot and fled with his servants to Jerusalem. There the tribes of Judah and Benjamin greeted him.

"We will always be loyal to the house of David," they swore.

Meanwhile in Shechem the ten tribes of Israel proclaimed Jeroboam king.

"Long live King Jeroboam!" they shouted. "Long live King Jeroboam!"

The kingdom of Saul, David and Solomon had been divided into two separate countries.

Rehoboam, the son of Solomon, reigned in Jerusalem over the kingdom of Judah. Jeroboam reigned in the north over the ten tribes of Israel.

EXERCISES

I. True or false? (Review section 1, pages 187 to 188.)

1. The people willingly worked in Solomon's labor force.

2. Solomon taxed the people very heavily.

3. Samuel advised the people to choose a king.

4. Solomon built altars to false gods for his wives.
5. God said that part of the kingdom would be taken from the house of David.

II. Complete each sentence. (Review section 2, pages 189 to 190.)

Ahijah, David, Ephraim, Jeroboam, Solomon

1. Jeroboam was put in charge of the forced labor for the tribe of _____.
2. _____ told Jeroboam he would rule over ten tribes.
3. The son of _____ would rule over two tribes.
4. God would not take the entire kingdom away for the sake of _____.
5. _____ fled to Egypt.

III. Fill in the correct name—Jeroboam or Rehoboam. (Review section 3, pages 190 to 192.)

1. _____ returned from Egypt.
2. _____, the son of Solomon, became the new king.
3. _____ told the people he would place heavy burdens upon them.
4. The people rebelled against _____.
5. _____ became king of the ten tribes of Israel.

IV. Questions for discussion:

1. What were the people's complaints against Solomon?
2. Why didn't the ten tribes rebel against Solomon?
3. What did the people of the north still have in common with the people of Judah, even though they now lived in different countries?
4. Compare Israel's Civil War with the American Civil War.

THINGS TO DO

1. *Proverb*—Make a poster on which you will print one of the proverbs of Solomon or a sentence from one of the psalms of David.

The best posters may be used to decorate the walls of the room.

2. *Council of Ten Tribes*—Pretend you are a delegate from one of the ten tribes to a council. Discuss what demands should be made of the new king, Rehoboam. Decide on what measures to take if he refuses these demands.

GUESS THE LETTER—A GAME

The leader writes the last letter of a name from Jewish history on the board. Lines are drawn to show the missing letters in the name.

If the leader chose Jerusalem, he would write:

_ _ _ _ _ _ _ _ m

The students then guess what letters are to be added. If the letter is found in the name, the leader writes it on the board in the proper space.

The students try to guess the letters with as few chances as possible.

CHAPTER XVIII

ELIJAH THE PROPHET

I. KINGS OF ISRAEL

ELIJAH was born a few years after the death of Solomon. Gone were the great days when David and Solomon had reigned in Jerusalem over a united nation.

Elijah was born in a small village named Thisbe, in Gilead, the section east of the Jordan where the 2 ½ tribes had settled.

As a child Elijah often heard of King Jeroboam who reigned in Shechem over the ten tribes of Israel. Elijah's teachers were angry when they heard how Jeroboam sinned against God.

"If the people go to Jerusalem to worship God," thought Jeroboam, "they will forget me and serve the house of David once more."

Jeroboam proclaimed that nobody was allowed to go to the Temple in Jerusalem. Instead he set up a golden calf in the city of Beth-El, where Jacob, after his dream, had once built an altar to God. Another golden calf was set up in Dan, the city at the northern border of Israel.

"These are your gods, O Israel, who brought you out of the land of Egypt," he declared.

Jeroboam was king for 22 years. Two years after his death, his son was killed in a plot.

Elijah was sure that Jeroboam's house was removed from the throne because of their sins.

One king followed another. The capital was changed from Shechem to the city of Samaria. But there was no improvement.

Elijah crossed the Jordan and joined a school of prophets who taught the word of God. His friends called him Elijah the Tishbite after the village of Thisbe where he had been born.

At last a new king named Ahab was crowned ruler of the 10 tribes of Israel.

"Maybe he will follow God," thought Elijah.

2. THE WORSHIP OF BAAL

Alas, things grew worse. Ahab married Jezebel, the daughter of a Phoenician king. Jezebel's father had once been high priest in the temple of the idol, Baal.

Jezebel lost no time in building a temple to Baal in the capital city of Samaria. Here the priests of Baal carried out the disgusting worship of Baal. Part of the worship consisted of cutting their flesh with knives, until the hands and bodies and faces of the worshipers were covered with blood. Sometimes a human being was sacrificed to the idol.

Many who worshiped God or who refused to kneel to the idol Baal were put to death.

ELIJAH ACCUSES AHAB

"Woe unto Jezebel and Ahab!" cried Elijah. "God will punish Israel for its sins. God will send a famine and there will be no bread to eat or water to drink."

Jezebel tried to capture Elijah but he escaped into the wilderness. Soon Israel was plagued with a famine.

Those who still worshiped God began to take heart when they heard how Elijah had defied wicked Jezebel. Legends began to spread among the people about this wonderful man.

"He is fed by the birds of the air," they said. "The ravens bring him bread and meat."

They told how he blessed a kind widow with the blessing that flour would always be found in her jar and oil in her pitcher. Even during the famine the flour and oil were never spent. The widow's son had been nursed back to health by Elijah after all hope was gone.

The famine was so severe that Ahab at last ordered, "Search every corner of the land until Elijah is found. Let him pray for rain so that the famine will come to an end."

Soon Elijah, clad in his flowing desert mantle which was tied with a thick leather belt around his waist, stood before Ahab.

"Let the false prophets of Baal prepare an altar unto Baal on Mount Carmel," said Elijah. "I shall prepare a sacrifice unto the true God."

450 priests of Baal gathered on Mount Carmel for a trial of fire with Elijah.

"O Baal," called the priests, "answer us."

But no fire descended from heaven.

When Elijah called upon God, fire descended and consumed the sacrifice.

All shouted, "The Lord, He is God! The Lord, He is God!"

The people began to battle the priests of Baal, many of whom were slain that day.

And Elijah said to Ahab, "Make ready your chariot. Return to your palace, for I hear the sound of rain."

Elijah ordered his servant to climb on the mountain to watch for clouds over the sea. Six times the servant went and returned.

"There is nothing," he said.

But the seventh time the servant said, "I see a cloud as small as a man's hand."

Soon the heaven was black with clouds. A strong wind blew, and the rains came down. The famine was over!

3. THE STILL SMALL VOICE

When Jezebel heard that many of the priests of Baal had been slain she grew very angry.

"Elijah will pay with his life," said Jezebel.

The prophet fled to Beersheba in Judah. From there he went into the wilderness, and then journeyed for 40 days and nights. At last he reached Mount Sinai where hundreds of years before Moses had received the ten commandments.

Elijah found a cave in Mount Sinai and lodged there. And God appeared unto Elijah.

"What is your wish?" asked the voice of God,

"The children of Israel have forgotten their covenant with God," said Elijah. "Your prophets have been slain with the sword, and only I am left. Now the wicked Jezebel seeks my life."

"Go forth," said the voice of God, "and stand upon the mount before the Lord."

Elijah climbed the mountain where once Moses had stood.

Suddenly a strong wind blew. The wind tore rocks from their places and shook the mountain. But God was not in the wind.

After the wind came an earthquake. The earth trembled. The mountain was split in two. But God was not in the earthquake.

A fire raged and burned furiously. But God was not in the fire.

After the fire, Elijah heard a still, small voice. And Elijah knew that God was in the still, small voice.

And God said, "Return and pick Elisha to be your pupil, and to serve as prophet after you. And he will anoint a new king in Syria to fight against the house of Ahab, and a new king to reign in Samaria. They will destroy those who have kneeled before Baal."

Elijah returned to Israel and found Elisha following the oxen in the field. Elijah approached Elisha and cast his mantle over him.

Elisha understood what the prophet with the long, gray beard meant.

"Let me kiss my parents farewell," said Elisha, "and then I shall follow you."

Elisha slew a pair of oxen, and invited his neighbors to a farewell feast.

After that he followed the prophet Elijah and fought against the worship of Baal.

4. THE VINEYARD OF NABOTH

Not far from Ahab's palace in the valley of Jezreel was a beautiful vineyard.

And Ahab spoke to Naboth, the owner of the vineyard, "Sell me your vineyard since it is close to my palace. I should like to use the land for a herb garden. In place of the vineyard I can pay you a good price, or give you an even better vineyard."

"God forbid that I should sell my inheritance," replied Naboth. "Were we not commanded to pass on our land from father to son?"

Ahab was greatly displeased because of Naboth's refusal to sell the vineyard.

When Jezebel saw that Ahab was downcast, she asked, "What is wrong?"

Ahab told her about Naboth's reply to his request.

"Do you call yourself a king?" demanded Jezebel. "In Phoenicia we know how to deal with such traitors to the king. The vineyard will be yours. I shall see to that."

Jezebel then wrote to the nobles in Naboth's city saying, "Hire two witnesses to swear that they heard Naboth curse the king."

Jezebel sealed the letter with the king's seal.

The nobles hired two witnesses who appeared in court and swore, "We heard Naboth curse the king."

"Treason," said the judges. "Let Naboth be put to death, and let his property be confiscated by the king."

Naboth was then stoned to death.

Ahab joyfully went down to the valley of Jezreel to take possession of the vineyard.

The word of God came to Elijah who was still in hiding: "Go down to Ahab in the valley of Jezreel and warn him that in the place where Naboth was slain, he will be slain. The dogs will lick his blood, and the birds of the air will devour the flesh of the wicked Jezebel."

As Ahab walked through the vineyard he was surprised to see the gray-bearded prophet standing before him. "Have you found me, my enemy?" asked Ahab.

"I have found you because you have done evil in the sight of God," replied Elijah. "Have you killed and also stolen what belonged to your victim, Naboth? On this spot will you be slain. The dogs will lick up your blood, and the birds of the air will devour the flesh of the wicked Jezebel."

In those days there was war between Syria and Israel. King Ahab fought disguised as a plain soldier. An arrow shot from a Syrian bow lodged between Ahab's lower armor and his breastplate.

"Carry me away from the battle," cried Ahab to the driver of the chariot. "I am severely wounded."

Ahab's life-blood oozed away, and the king was dead before the chariot reached his palace.

The servants washed the chariot in Jezreel, and the dogs licked the blood as Elijah had warned.

Elisha carried out the second part of his master's prophecy.

Spurred on by Elisha, a captain in the army of Israel named Jehu rebelled against Ahab's son. Jezebel and her son were slain in the rebellion.

"Give Jezebel decent burial," commanded Jehu after the fighting was over. "After all, she was a queen."

When the servants searched for Jezebel's body, they discovered that her flesh had been eaten by the birds of the air.

Thus the house of Ahab was punished for its sin against Naboth, and for its cruelty against the worshipers of God.

The new king, Jehu, destroyed the temple of Baal. He finished the work of Elijah and Elisha who had saved Israel from the religion of Baal worship.

5. THE LEGEND OF ELIJAH

Nobody saw Elijah die. People said that as Elijah and Elisha walked together a chariot of fire appeared drawn by horses of fire. Elijah went up in the chariot like a whirlwind into heaven.

According to the legend, Elijah never died. He comes back from heaven to help people who are in trouble.

On Passover Elijah visits every Jewish home. A special cup, called *Kos Eleeyahu,* or "Elijah's cup" is filled with wine and set aside for the prophet.

After the festive *Seder* meal the door is opened to welcome *Eleeyahu Ha-Navi* (Elijah the prophet). All join in singing.

Eleeyahu Ha-Navi
Eleeyahu Ha-Tishbi
Eleeyahu, Eleeyahu, Eleeyahu Ha-Giladi

At every *brith*, a chair is reserved for Elijah the prophet who comes to bless the new-born boy.

Elijah is the friend of all who are poor or who are in trouble.

Once, so the legend goes, Elijah appeared in the form of an old Arab to a farmer who had lost his wealth. The farmer was so poor that he now worked in the field of another farmer.

"You are destined to enjoy seven good years," said Elijah. "When do you want them—now, or in the closing years of your life?"

At first the man turned aside not believing Elijah's words. But after Elijah repeated the question several times, the man said, "I shall ask my wife for advice."

When Elijah returned, the man said, "My wife and I have decided that we want the seven good years to come at once."

"Go home," replied the prophet. "Before you cross the threshold your good fortune will have filled your house."

When the man approached his house, his wife came to tell him that his children had found a treasure in the ground.

"Let us use the money wisely," said his wife. "Let us practise charity, and help the poor."

For seven years they lived modestly. They gave money to the poor and helped many worthy causes. Only a small part of the fortune did they use for themselves.

After seven years Elijah appeared to announce that the money must be returned.

"I should like to consult my wife again," the man said.

"Tell the old man," his wife advised, "that we shall willingly return the fortune if he can find somebody who will make better use of the fortune than we did."

"You may keep this wealth as long as you live," replied Elijah, "for you have used this money unselfishly and have helped all who were in need."

Suddenly the old Arab disappeared and the man knew that he had been helped by Elijah the prophet.

Once Elijah appeared in the form of a magician to help an old couple that had no money to buy *matzah* and wine for Passover. Their home was in darkness for they could not afford even candles.

"May I join you for the *Seder?*" asked the magician.

"But we have no food or *matzah* or wine," replied the old couple.

"Nonsense", laughed the magician, "I shall take care of that."

The magician raised his hand. "Hocus, Pocus, let there be light!" said the magician.

In the twinkling of an eye candles appeared.

"Hocus, Pocus, let there be *matzah*, wine, meat, soup."

Soon there was a royal feast spread before the surprised old couple.

They ran to ask the Rabbi whether they were permitted to partake of the magician's food. The Rabbi said that it was allowed.

When they returned the magician had disappeared, and they knew that they had really been helped by Elijah the prophet.

It is Elijah who brings together children and parents who have been separated.

It is Elijah who will some day announce the Messiah, the anointed prince of God who will usher in a perfect world.

Three days before the coming of the Messiah, the prophet will call out, "Let there be peace on earth!"

On the second day, Elijah will call out, "Let all wickedness disappear from the earth."

On the last day, Elijah will announce, "Salvation will come upon earth!"

The trumpet will be sounded, Elijah will introduce the Messiah and mankind will enjoy perfect happiness on earth.

Of course, these are only legends. The legends are beautiful, however, because they show our faith in a better world. To the Jew, Elijah is a symbol that we must help others in need, and that we must work for a world at peace.

EXERCISES

I. Arrange in the order in which these events happened. (Review sections 1 and 2, pages 195 to 199.)

1. A new king named Ahab was crowned ruler over the ten tribes of Israel.
2. Jeroboam proclaimed that nobody could visit the Temple in Jerusalem.
3. Elijah said to Ahab, "Return to your palace for I hear the sound of rain."
4. The priests of Baal gathered for a trial by fire with Elijah.
5. Israel was plagued with a famine.
6. Jezebel built a temple to Baal.
7. When Elijah called upon God, fire descended from heaven and consumed the sacrifice.

II. Choose the correct name or phrase. (Review section 3, pages 199 to 201.)
1. Jezebel wanted to kill _____. (Ahab, Elijah)
2. Elijah went to Mount _____. (Sinai, Tabor)
3. God appeared to Elijah in the _____. (still small voice, wind)
4. God told Elijah to pick Elisha as the new _____. (king, prophet)
5. Elisha was a _____ before he followed Elijah. (farmer, shepherd)

III. Match. (Review section 4, pages 201 to 203.)

Column A	Column B
Ahab	1. Owner of vineyard
Elijah	2. Captain who rebelled against king and queen
Jehu	3. Wanted vineyard
Jezebel	4. Warned king and queen of punishment
Naboth	5. Wrote to nobles to kill innocent man

IV. List 4 legends about Elijah in a sentence for each legend. (Review section 5, pages 203 to 206.)

V. Questions for discussion:
1. Compare Elijah and Nathan.
2. Which legend about Elijah do you like most? Why?
3. Suggest another title for this chapter.

THINGS TO DO

1. *Story Hour*—Find a legend about Elijah in a story book or in a book of legends. Tell the story to the class.

2. *Songs*—Learn a song about Elijah. Two favorites are:
1. *Eleeyahu Ha-Navi*
2. *Al S'fat Yam Kinneret*

3. *Haggadah*—Make a picture *Haggadah*. Include a picture of Elijah's cup, opening the door for Elijah, Elijah the prophet, the words of the song *Eleeyahu Ha-Navi*.

Other pictures that might be included are: reciting the Four Questions; the Passover plate; the taskmasters; crossing the Red Sea; in the desert; Moses at Sinai; a decoration for the song *Chad Gadya*.

MUSIC MEMORY QUIZ

Play songs about Elijah, Passover songs, other holiday songs, synagogue songs, or Israeli songs on the piano or on the phonograph.

Each student must list the name or the first line of the song. The one who lists the most names correctly is the winner.

CHAPTER XIX

JONAH AND THE MESSAGE
OF FORGIVENESS

1. JONAH'S FLIGHT FROM GOD

ELISHA followed in the footsteps of his master, Elijah the prophet. Many pupils came to Elisha to learn the word of God.

One of the pupils of Elisha was a prophet named Jonah. His story is one of the strangest stories in the Bible.

Jonah was born in a small village not far from the *Kinneret* or Sea of Galilee. Jonah prophesied that Israel would be victorious against its enemies. His prophecy came true and, for a while, Israel regained some of its lost power.

One day the word of the Lord came to Jonah saying, "Arise, go to Nineveh, the capital of Assyria. Proclaim that the city will be destroyed because the people are so wicked."

And Jonah thought, "If the people repent, God will

pardon them and not destroy the city. Then I shall be called a false prophet. Better for me to run away."

Jonah went to the port of Jaffa where he found a ship going to the land of Tarshish.

"What is the fare for passage to Tarshish?" he asked.

He paid the fare requested, and set sail on the boat.

When the ship was in the midst of the sea a great storm came up. A strong wind tossed the ship from side to side, and the waves almost broke the boat in two.

"Pray for your lives," shouted the captain.

Meanwhile, the sailors were ordered to throw the merchandise overboard to lighten the ship.

Jonah had gone down to an inner cabin in the boat where he slept.

"Wake up," cried the shipmaster. "Do you not see that we are in danger? Pray that we may be saved."

Jonah climbed to the top deck where the sailors were casting lots to find out whose deed had angered Heaven. The lot fell upon Jonah.

"Who are you?" demanded the sailors.

"I am a Hebrew," replied Jonah, "and I worship the Lord, the God of heaven, who has made the sea and the dry land. This storm is a punishment because I tried to flee from God."

"What can we do so that the sea may be calm?" they asked. The tempest, indeed, had grown more severe.

And Jonah said, "Take me and cast me into the sea."

"Let us row hard. Perhaps we can reach land," ordered the captain.

JONAH: "I AM A HEBREW"

When the sailors saw that it was hopeless they decided to cast Jonah into the sea.

"We pray, O Lord, that You will not hold us guilty of shedding innocent blood. We do this to save our lives at the request of Jonah himself."

The sailors then cast Jonah into the sea. Immediately, the wind died down and the sea became calm.

At that moment a giant fish swam past the boat. Poor Jonah was swallowed alive.

But three days later the fish vomited out Jonah upon dry land.

2. IN THE CITY OF NINEVEH

Once more the word of God came to Jonah, "Arise, go to Nineveh and proclaim that the city will be destroyed because of its wickedness."

Jonah traveled to the land of Assyria until he came to the capital city of Nineveh.

The prophet walked through the city and called out, "In forty more days, Nineveh will be destroyed by God because of its wickedness! In forty more days, Nineveh will be overthrown!"

"Let us pray for forgiveness," said the people of Nineveh. "This man is a prophet of God and he speaks the truth."

The people covered their heads with ashes and their bodies with sackcloth as a sign of mourning.

"What is wrong?" the king of Nineveh asked his servants. "Why do the people wear sackcloth and ashes?"

"A prophet of God has come from Israel to prophesy that our city will be destroyed because of our wicked deeds," replied the servants.

"Woe unto us!" cried out the king. "Surely God will destroy us because of our sins. Let us proclaim a day of fasting. Let neither man nor beast taste any food or drink any water. Let us pray unto God for forgiveness. Let us turn from our evil ways. Maybe God will pardon our sins."

The king's decree was proclaimed in all the streets of Nineveh.

When the appointed day of fasting came, neither man nor beast tasted food or drank water. The people covered themselves again with sackcloth and with ashes.

"Forgive us, O God," prayed the king and his subjects. "Pardon our sins and we will sin no more!"

3. THE MESSAGE OF FORGIVENESS

The people of Nineveh searched their hearts. They knew that they had stolen, lied, cheated, shed blood. The king appointed honest judges to judge wisely, and officers to provide for the widow, the orphan and the poor.

When God saw that the people repented, He pardoned their sins.

But Jonah was very angry.

"I shall be called a false prophet," he said. "Was not this the reason for my flight to Tarshish? For I know that God is merciful and forgiving."

Then Jonah went out of the city to see what would

happen to Nineveh. The hot, oriental sun beat down on the prophet's head. The glare of the sun on the white sand blinded the prophet.

God prepared a vegetable plant which grew over-night. Jonah sat in the shadow of the plant and found relief from the burning sun. The next morning, however, a worm ate the leaves of the plant. Again Jonah was tortured by the scorching sun and the merciless hot east wind of the desert.

"Why has this plant been taken from me?" asked Jonah. "Take my life, O Lord, for it is better for me to die than to live."

"Are you very angry because of the plant?" asked God.

"I am angry even unto death," replied Jonah.

"You want Me to spare the plant which came up in a night and which withered in a night," said God. "But you don't want Me to take pity on this great city with its thousands of innocent people. God does not want the sinner to die, only to repent from evil and to do good."

"But what shall I say when I am accused of being a false prophet?" demanded Jonah.

"Teach the people that the true prophet's message is a message not only of punishment but of forgiveness."

Jonah returned to Israel to teach the message of forgiveness.

Students often argue about whether Jonah could have been swallowed alive by a whale. Some say that the incident about the whale is only a legend.

Of course, this is not the important part of the story.

The story of Jonah teaches us many important lessons.

Jonah learned that one cannot run away from God or from one's duty. He learned that God takes pity on people of all nations, for Nineveh was in a different country.

He learned that fasting is not enough. People must change their wicked habits.

He learned also that God is a God of love who forgives when people repent.

On Yom Kippur, the Day of Atonement, the beautiful book of Jonah is read in the synagogue.

In the afternoon of this holy day of fasting, as the sun begins to set, the worshipers listen carefully to the story of Jonah.

"We fast to show that we are sorry for any wrong we may have done," the worshipers think to themselves. "We pray to God that He will forgive our sins, and that He will guide us to do what is right in the future."

EXERCISES

I. Who said to whom? (Review section 1, pages 209 to 212.)

   1. "Arise, go to Nineveh, the capital of Assyria. Proclaim that the city will be destroyed because the people are so wicked."
   2. "Wake up. Do you not see that we are in danger?"
   3. "I am a Hebrew, and I worship the Lord, the God of heaven who has made the sea and the dry land."
   4. "Let us row hard. Perhaps we can reach land."
   5. "We pray, O Lord, that You will not hold us guilty of shedding innocent blood."

II. True or false? (Review section 2, pages 212 to 213.)
1. Nineveh was the capital of Israel.
2. Jonah proclaimed, "In forty more days, Nineveh will be destroyed by God because of its wickedness."
3. The people made fun of Jonah.
4. The people prayed to God for forgiveness.

III. Why? (Review section 3, pages 213 to 215.)
1. Why did God pardon the people of Nineveh?
2. Why did Jonah wait outside of the city?
3. Why did the plant wither?
4. Why was Jonah angry when the plant withered?
5. Why did Jonah run away to Tarshish at first instead of going to Nineveh?

IV. Questions for discussion:
1. Which is the most important lesson taught by the book of Jonah? Why?
2. Why is Jonah read on Yom Kippur?
3. Why is Yom Kippur the holiest day of the year? Mention some prayers recited on Yom Kippur.

THINGS TO DO

1. *Research*—Report to the class about the boats used in ancient times.

2. *Holiday Scrap-book*—Add to your holiday scrap-book pictures dealing with Yom Kippur. Here are some suggestions: a. a worshiper in prayer shawl; b. the procession with the Torah; c. the blast of the shofar marking the end of the fast; d. a greeting card extending best wishes for the coming year; e. Jonah on the boat; f. Jonah in Nineveh; g. the High Priest and the Temple

3. *Composition*—Jonah told the sailors, "I am a Hebrew."

Write a composition using these words as the title, 'I Am a Hebrew."

FINISH THE JINGLE

Jonah was told to prophesy
That Nineveh's wicked would surely ————.

From God and duty he tried to flee,
And so he ran away to ————.

When the sailors cast him over the rail
He was swallowed alive by a giant ————.

Then Jonah on his mission went,
And all the people began to ————.

The king and his subjects were overjoyed
Because their city was not ————.

UNIT SIX

The Prophets of Judah

CHAPTER XX

ISAIAH

1. IN JERUSALEM

ISAIAH was born in Jerusalem a few years after the death of Jonah.

Isaiah's father was a noble, and so Isaiah knew the princes and the nobles of Jerusalem. But he also knew the poor people of Jerusalem. Often he would walk among the crude houses made of mud where the poor lived. He pitied them and hoped to help them some day.

A descendant of David and Solomon ruled as king in Jerusalem. The king lived in the great palace, but he had been ill and so did not take an active interest in the problems of the people.

One day Isaiah wandered to the gate of Jerusalem. A trial was going on. Isaiah listened.

"I am a farmer," Isaiah heard the first man say to the judge. "I owe my neighbor money for food and seed which he lent me. I cannot pay it back now because I have been too ill to work my land. But next year I can pay it back."

"He promised to give me the money or his field," replied the second man. "I refuse to wait until next year for the money he owes me."

"Do you have a son?" asked the judge.

"I do," replied the farmer.

"Sell him as a slave for six years. In that way you can obtain money to pay your debt."

"That I will never do."

"Then you must forfeit your field," ruled the judge.

Isaiah shook his head sadly. Each day he witnessed scenes like this. He knew the judge well and knew that he took bribes from the rich to decide in their favor.

Surely God would punish Judah if such wickedness continued!

Isaiah walked past the king's palace.

A crowd had gathered. They were shouting, "Bread! Give us bread!"

Isaiah saw many old, sick people in the crowd.

One woman called out, "I am a widow! Give me bread for my children!"

Soldiers soon appeared in front of the palace gate and forced the crowd to scatter.

"Did not Moses command that we take care of the poor?" thought Isaiah.

Greatly troubled, he turned toward the Temple court.

2. "HOLY, HOLY, HOLY"

Isaiah walked through the long Temple court and entered the Temple.

A *Kohen*, or priest, had just left the altar where a sacrifice had been offered to God. A small flame flickered from time to time. The coals were still hot.

Now all was quiet. The Temple was empty.

Isaiah watched the sparks fly upward. Suddenly the very heavens seemed to open. There was a majestic throne on which the Lord was seated.

Around the throne flew winged angels. And the angels called out to each other:

> "Holy, holy, holy is the Lord of hosts;
> The whole earth is full of His glory."

The posts of the Temple seemed to tremble as the angels sang their song of praise to God. Smoke filled the Temple and hid Isaiah from the outside world.

In fear Isaiah called out:

> "Woe is me! for I am undone;
> Because I am a man of unclean lips,
> And I dwell in the midst of a people of unclean
>   lips;
> For mine eyes have seen the King,
> The Lord of hosts."

One of the angels flew to the altar. With a pair of tongs he picked up a glowing coal from the altar. He touched Isaiah's mouth with the hot coal.

"This coal has touched your lips," Isaiah heard the angel say, "and has burned away your sins."

Then God said, "Whom shall I send? Who will go for us?"

"Here am I," replied Isaiah; "send me."

And God said, "Go tell the people that Israel and Judah will be punished because of their sins. But those who are righteous will remain to rebuild the cities that have been destroyed."

Suddenly the vision disappeared. Isaiah looked around. All was the same as before in the Temple, but the coals had grown cold.

Isaiah knew that he must devote the rest of his life to teaching the word of God.

3. THE TEACHINGS OF THE PROPHET

Each day Isaiah walked through the streets of Jerusalem telling the people to change their ways.

Isaiah remembered how the rich farmer had taken his neighbor's field. He had joined two fields together, and now was the owner of both.

Isaiah went to the gate of the city and called out in the presence of the judge and the people:

> "Woe unto them that join house to house,
> That lay field to field!"

Often Isaiah would speak to the crowds that entered the Temple.

"Hear the words of God," said the prophet:

> "When you spread forth your hands,
> I will hide My eyes from you;
> Yea, when you make many prayers,
> I will not hear;
> Your hands are full of blood.

Wash you, make you clean,
Put away the evil of your doings
From before My eyes.
Cease to do evil.

Learn to do well,
Seek justice,
Relieve the oppressed,
Judge the fatherless,
Plead for the widow."

When the holiest day of the year, Yom Kippur, came, the men and women of Judah gathered in the Temple. They offered sacrifices, fasted and prayed to God.

"Why have we fasted, but You do not answer our prayer?" called out the people to God.

"God doesn't want sacrifices," replied Isaiah. "He wants justice and kindness."

Isaiah taught the people that their fasting did not mean anything unless they took to heart the teachings of the Torah.

"What kind of fast day does God want?" asked the people.

The prophet replied:

"Is it not to deal your bread to the hungry,
    And that you bring the poor that are cast out to
        your house?
When you see the naked that you cover him
And that you hide not yourself from your own
    flesh.

Then shall your light break forth as the morning,
And your healing shall spring forth speedily."

The people listened to the words of Isaiah, and little
by little they began to understand that God wants not
sacrifices but justice.

EXERCISES

I. Choose the correct name or phrase. (Review section 1,
   pages 221 to 222.)
   1. Isaiah was born in _____. (Jerusalem, Samaria)
   2. Isaiah was the son of a _____. (noble, slave)
   3. The judge decided in favor of the_____. (poor
      farmer, rich farmer)
   4. Isaiah knew that the judge was _____. (dishonest,
      honest)
   5. The people outside of the palace demanded _____.
      (bread, war)

II. Complete each sentence. (Review section 2, pages 222 to
    224.)
    angels, altar, Isaiah, *Kohen*, Temple
    1. Isaiah saw a vision of God in the _____.
    2. The sacrifice had been prepared by a _____.
    3. The _____ sang, "Holy, holy, holy is the Lord of
       hosts."
    4. An angel touched Isaiah's lips with a coal from the
       _____.
    5. _____ said that he would teach the word of God.

III. Answer each question in a complete sentence. (Review
     section 3, pages 224 to 226.)
     1. Why was Isaiah angry at the rich farmer?

2. Why didn't God listen to the prayers of the people?
3. Which is the holiest day of the year?
4. What does God want instead of sacrifices?
5. Why is fasting not enough?

IV. Questions for discussion:

1. What is the difference between a fortune-teller and a prophet like Isaiah?
2. Isaiah's words about fasting are read in the synagogue on the morning of Yom Kippur; the story of Jonah is read in the afternoon of Yom Kippur. Compare the message of Jonah with the message of Isaiah.

THINGS TO DO

1. *Court Trial*—Act out the trial of the rich farmer and the poor farmer. Let there be three judges instead of one. The judges must arrive at a fair decision.

2. *Yom Kippur Service*—Learn some of the songs of the Yom Kippur service. Some suggestions are:

a. *Kadosh* ("Holy, Holy, Holy")
b. *S'lach Lanu*
c. *Avinu Malkenu*

Prepare to read with expression at the Junior Congregation service the speech of Isaiah about fasting or the story of Jonah.

WORD GAME

How many words can you find in the name "Jerusalem"? The fourth and fifth letters for example, spell out "us"; the last four letters when rearranged spell "meal", etc.

CHAPTER XXI

ISAIAH'S PROPHECY
OF PEACE

I. THE LOST TEN TRIBES

ISAIAH warned Israel and Judah that many would go into exile because of their sins.

He named his son "Shear-yashuv" which means "the remnant will return." He wanted to show that he had not lost all hope. He was sure that some day a few of the people who had been righteous would return to their land.

Isaiah was very sad when he heard of the sins of the ten tribes of Israel. The people still worshiped Baal and the two calves set up by Jeroboam. One king had even sacrificed his son to an idol by throwing him into the fire. The poor were neglected. Many of the Israelites were so poor that they had to sell themselves into slavery.

One day messengers ran to Ahaz, king of Judah, with the message, "Israel and Syria are sending an army against us!"

The kings of Israel and Syria marched up to the very

walls of Jerusalem. When the people of Judah heard of the invasion they trembled like the leaves of a tree in the wind.

The word of God came to Isaiah saying, "You and your son must go out to Ahaz, king of Judah. Tell him to keep calm, and not to fear Israel and Syria. For I am sending a strong nation against them."

Isaiah and his son went out to meet Ahaz, the king, and told him the word of God.

Soon news came that Assyria had attacked both Israel and Syria. The two kings withdrew from Jerusalem and paid a heavy tribute to Assyria.

Ahaz, king of Judah, rejoiced at the news. He, too, sent a rich present to the king of Assyria.

At that time a second son was born to Isaiah. The prophet called him "Maher-shalal" which means, "Quickly the spoil will fall into the hands of the enemy."

"Israel will quickly fall to the enemy," said Isaiah, "because of its attack on Jerusalem, and because of the sins of the people."

The king of Israel soon tried to rebel against Assyria. He sent messengers to Egypt asking for help against Assyria.

In anger the king of Assyria sent a large army against Samaria, the capital of the ten tribes of Israel.

The Israelites fought bravely for three years. But at last the city fell before the strong Assyrian army. Israel had fallen!

The king of Assyria exiled the ten tribes to Assyria

and to other countries. Many of the Israelites escaped to Jerusalem and settled in the cities of Judah.

Isaiah sadly told the people of Jerusalem, "Let this be a warning to Judah! Some day, however, God will bring back the remnant of the ten tribes to rebuild Israel."

Where did the ten tribes go? Nobody really knows.

Many strange legends have sprung up about the ten tribes. Some of the nations of Europe claimed to be descended from the lost ten tribes.

Others said, "The American Indians are the lost ten tribes."

According to a Jewish legend the ten tribes were exiled to the land of Sambatyon (Sabbath land). The land of Sambatyon lies beyond the mountains of darkness.

In order to enter this land one must cross the river of Sambatyon which constantly throws up large stones. Only on the Sabbath does the river rest.

Once a traveler lost his way and entered, by chance, the land of Sambatyon. Here he found the descendants of Ephraim and the other tribes. The children of the lost ten tribes were giants in stature and in strength.

They were waiting for the day when the children of Israel would return from the four corners of the world to the land of Israel. Then they, too, would rejoin the exiles who were seeking freedom in the land of their fathers.

2. THE SILOAM TUNNEL

The ten tribes of Israel had existed as a separate kingdom for 200 years after the death of Solomon. Even though Israel had fallen, the world would always remember the teachings of its prophets. Men like Elijah, Elisha and Jonah had taught the people to worship one God with pure hearts.

Would Judah be destroyed too? Isaiah taught the Jews that they had nothing to fear if only they obeyed the laws of God.

Ahaz was succeeded on the throne by his son, Hezekiah. The new king tried to be worthy of sitting on the throne of David. He removed the idols from the land, and judged his people wisely.

King Hezekiah called his officers and asked, "How can we strengthen our city? In case of siege we do not have enough water for the people of Jerusalem."

"Let us build a tunnel," advised his officers, "that will connect the fountain of Siloam, which is outside the wall, with the inner city."

King Hezekiah began to build the tunnel. Never, since the days of King Solomon, had such a great task been carried out by the king.

The miners began to cut through the rock from both ends with stone picks. They worked long and hard.

At last, after many months of hard work, the miners who began working from inside the city heard voices.

"Soon we shall meet the other miners," they shouted with joy.

Both groups of miners lifted their picks. There was a split in the rock, and the two groups of miners stood face to face. The tunnel had been completed. The waters began to flow into Jerusalem.

A Hebrew inscription was placed on the rock at the point where the two groups of miners met.

This inscription was found, almost 100 years ago, by an Arab boy who waded in the waters of the tunnel looking for excitement. It is one of our most precious ancient inscriptions.

3. JUDAH IS SAVED!

The king's preparations for a siege were wise indeed. Soon the Assyrian army swept down on Judah like a wolf attacking a flock of sheep.

City after city fell before Sennacherib, the king of Assyria. Would Jerusalem fall too?

The king of Assyria sent one of his generals to the walls of Jerusalem with a demand for surrender. Above, on the walls, stood the soldiers of Hezekiah.

"Why do you resist?" shouted the Assyrian general in Hebrew. "You can't fight against one of our captains, and here you try to resist our whole army."

"Leave our city," said Hezekiah's officers, "and we are willing to pay a yearly tax."

"Nonsense," replied the Assyrian general. "Where are your soldiers that you try to argue with me? I'll wager that if I gave you 2000 horses you couldn't find riders for these horses. Surrender before it is too late!"

The citizens of Jerusalem in great terror crowded around the wall and listened to the Assyrian general's boastful words.

"Woe is us!" cried the people. "All of us will die at the hands of the Assyrians."

"The people are losing courage," whispered the officers to each other. "Let us ask the Assyrians to speak in a language that the people do not understand."

"Talk to us in your own language," said the officers to the Assyrians. "Do not talk to us in Hebrew for all these people are listening."

"That is just what we want," shouted the general in Hebrew. "We want them to know that they will all die at the point of the sword, unless Hezekiah surrenders Jerusalem to us."

In great fear the officers reported what they had heard to the king.

Hezekiah entered the Temple and prayed to God for help. He sent for the prophet Isaiah for advice.

"Have no fear," advised Isaiah. "God will deliver Jerusalem from the hands of the Assyrians. Sennacherib will not conquer Jerusalem. Because he has lifted the sword against Judah he will die by the sword."

When Hezekiah's officers told the Assyrians that Jerusalem would not surrender, the Assyrian general was very angry.

"We leave you now, for first we will conquer Egypt," shouted the general. "But do not think that Egypt can save you. Soon we will return to destroy you."

Sennacherib left a large army in Judah, and attacked Egypt with the rest of his soldiers.

But a plague of mice invaded the Assyrian camp in Egypt. The mice gnawed at the bowstrings and at the Assyrian armor. Soon the bows and arrows were destroyed by the sharp teeth of the mice.

This was one army Sennacherib could not destroy—
an army of mice.

Sennacherib returned to his camp in Judah hoping to
attack Jerusalem.

But the army of mice was not through with its deadly
work. The mice began to spread disease.

The Assyrians died by the hundreds and by the thousands. Officers and soldiers alike fell before the dreaded
disease.

In panic the Assyrian army, led by King Sennacherib
and his generals, fled back to Nineveh.

Isaiah's prophecy had come true! Judah was saved!
Jerusalem had not fallen into the hands of the enemy!

Some time after Sennacherib had returned to Nineveh,
his sons slew him with a sword. The king who lifted a
sword against Jerusalem had died by the sword!

4. "NEITHER SHALL THEY LEARN WAR ANY MORE"

One day as Isaiah walked through the streets of Jerusalem, he stopped to speak to his friend, the blacksmith.

The smith blew air through the bellows to fan the fire.
The smith picked up some iron tools that lay in his shop
and heated them in the fire.

"What's that in your hand?" asked the prophet.

The smith held it up for the prophet to see. It was a
small plowshare which the farmer uses to cut the soil
and to turn it over.

"A plowshare," said Isaiah. "What are you doing with
it?"

"The blade will make an excellent sword," said the

blacksmith. "We need swords. We can't afford to use iron for tools."

The blacksmith held up another farmer's tool. It was a pair of pruning-hooks, a large pair of scissors used to cut the branches of trees.

"These pruning-hooks will make two spears," said the smith. "The king's officers will pay me a good price for these spears. We may need them soon. Who knows when the Assyrians will return."

"The Assyrians won't come back," replied the prophet smiling.

"Then it will be some other enemy," said the blacksmith. "Sooner or later we have war."

The blacksmith returned to his bellows and to the fire. The sparks flew upward as the smith forged weapons from the farmer's tools.

The sparks reminded Isaiah of the vision he had seen many years before in the Temple.

"Why must we have war?" thought Isaiah. "Why must nations go to war against each other? Why must brother kill brother? The real hero is not the warrior but the man who teaches his neighbors to live in peace."

Isaiah closed his eyes. Another vision seemed to unfold before him.

It was a vision of nations streaming to Jerusalem. From all corners of the world men and women came to Jerusalem.

They climbed Mount Zion and entered the Temple. There they prayed to God for peace.

With them they brought their swords, their spears and all their other weapons. They took their swords and beat them into plowshares. Their spears they beat into pruning-hooks.

"Instead of waging war we will till the soil, and each man shall live in safety," declared all the nations. "We will not lift up sword against our neighbors, nor will we learn war any more."

By this time a crowd had gathered in the blacksmith's shop. They recognized the prophet and asked for a message.

Isaiah turned to the men and women before him and said:

"And it shall come to pass in the end of days,
That the mountain of the Lord's house shall be es-
tablished as the top of the mountains,
And shall be exalted above the hills.
And all nations shall flow unto it.

And many peoples shall go and say,
'Come ye, and let us go up to the mountain of the
Lord,
To the house of the God of Jacob;
And He will teach us of His ways,
And we will walk in His paths.'
For out of Zion shall go forth the law,
And the word of the Lord from Jerusalem.

THE VISION OF ISAIAH: "AND THEY SHALL BEAT THEIR
SWORDS INTO PLOWSHARES"

And He shall judge between the nations,
And shall decide for many peoples.
And they shall beat their swords into plowshares,
And their spears into pruning-hooks;
Nation shall not lift up sword against nation,
Neither shall they learn war any more."

Thus spoke Isaiah, the great prophet of peace.

We hope that some day Isaiah's words will come true, and that nations will not wage war any more.

EXERCISES

I. Fill in the name of the correct country. (Review section 1, pages 228 to 230.)

Assyria, Israel, Judah, Syria

1. Isaiah called his son "Shear-yashuv" to show that the exiles of Israel and _____ would return to their land.
2. The ten tribes of _____ worshiped calves set up by Jeroboam.
3. _____ and Israel attacked Jerusalem.
4. Isaiah told the king of _____ that Jerusalem would be conquered.
5. _____ destroyed Israel.
6. According to the legend the lost ten tribes of _____ are in the land of Sambatyon.

II. True or false? (Review section 2, pages 230 to 232.)

1. The kingdom of the ten tribes of Israel existed for about 100 years after the death of Solomon.

2. We remember Israel because of the teachings of great prophets like Elijah, Elisha and Jonah.
3. Isaiah taught that Jerusalem would not fall even if the people sinned.
4. King Hezekiah built the tunnel of Siloam so that water could be brought from the fountain of Siloam to Jerusalem.
5. An inscription in Hebrew was placed in the tunnel at the point where the two groups of miners met.

III. Who said to whom? (Review section 3, pages 232 to 234.)
   1. "Why do you resist?"
   2. "Leave our city, and we are willing to pay a yearly tax."
   3. "The people are losing courage. Let us ask the Assyrian to speak in a language that the people do not understand."
   4. "God will deliver Jerusalem from the hands of the Assyrians."
   5. "We leave you now, for first we will conquer Egypt."

IV. Choose the correct name or phrase. (Review section 4, pages 234 to 238.)
   1. _____ is called the prophet of peace. (Isaiah, Jonah)
   2. Isaiah believed that world peace would come _____. (in a few years, after many years)
   3. Nations would come to the _____. (king's palace, Temple)
   4. God's word would be heard in _____. (Jerusalem, Nineveh)
   5. Nations would beat their swords into _____. (plowshares, spears)

V. Questions for discussion:
>   1. Which kingdom was really stronger—Israel or Judah?
>   Why?
>   2. In your opinion, where are the lost ten tribes?
>   3. What events in Isaiah's life made him look forward
>   to the time when the nations would be at peace?

THINGS TO DO

1. *Memory Gem*—Memorize Isaiah's prophecy of peace or one of his other prophecies.

2. *Memorial Day Poster*—Draw a poster for Memorial Day or for Armistice Day using a quotation from Isaiah.

3. *United Nations Peace Council*—Pretend that each student is a delegate of one of the member nations of the United Nations.

Arrange a conference on ways of preventing war.

4. *Research*—Locate on the map:

> a. Damascus, capital of Syria
> b. Assyria (east of the Tigris River).

A CALENDAR PROBLEM

Samaria, the capital of Israel, was destroyed by Assyria in 722 B.C.E. (Before the Common Era).

How many years ago did this happen?

CHAPTER XXII

JEREMIAH —
THE PROPHET OF SORROW

I. AN UNJUST RULER

THE PROPHET Isaiah foresaw the fall of Israel. The prophet Jeremiah foresaw the fall of Judah. There had been peace for many years after the days of Isaiah and King Hezekiah. Mighty Assyria fell and was no more, but Jerusalem remained strong.

"Peace, peace," said the leaders of Judah. "There will always be peace for Judah. The city of Jerusalem can never fall."

"You say that there will be peace," replied the prophet Jeremiah, "but I say that there is no peace unless you obey the laws of God."

The prophet knew that the king, whose name was Jehoiakim, was a wicked king.

Jeremiah was sad when he saw what was happening in Jerusalem. Rich men made their poor neighbors serve as slaves. Judges were dishonest and favored those who gave them bribes. The king himself encouraged the worship of idols.

One day Jeremiah passed King Jehoiakim's palace and found some men tied to the stocks and to the pillory.

"Why have you been placed here?" asked the prophet. "What wrong have you done?"

"Wrong?" replied one of the men. "Our crime was that we asked to be paid our just wages!"

"Who would not pay you?" asked Jeremiah.

"The king!" answered another prisoner. "Look at the beautiful cedar palace in which our king lives. We helped decorate the rooms of the palace and were promised good wages. But when we asked to be paid, the king's officers shouted that every subject owes the king the duty of serving without pay. We demanded the right to see the king, but were placed in the stocks instead."

The prophet sadly shook his head. A crowd had gathered as Jeremiah spoke to the prisoners. Speaking in a loud voice so that all could hear, the prophet said:

"Woe unto him that builds his house by unright-
    eousness,
And his chambers by injustice
That uses his neighbor's service without wages,
And gives him not his hire;
That says, 'I will build me a wide house
And spacious chambers,'
And cuts him out windows,
And it is ceiled with cedar, and painted with bright
    red.

Will you reign because you strive to excel in cedar?
Did not your father eat and drink, and do justice
    and righteousness?
Then it was well with him.
He judged the cause of the poor and needy.
Then it was well.
Is not this to know Me? says the Lord."

2. A SINFUL NATION

One day Jeremiah met a Hebrew slave in the market-place not far from the gate of Jerusalem. The slave greeted Jeremiah.

The prophet looked closely and recognized a farmer who had once owned a field in his native village. He had not seen him for many years.

"Alas, Jeremiah, I have sunk very low," said the slave.

"What happened to your field and house?" asked the prophet.

"I lost them in the years of the drought. I borrowed and borrowed and borrowed. When I could not pay back my field was taken, and the judge ruled that I must serve as a slave."

"How long have you served your master?" asked Jeremiah.

"Almost ten years."

"Ten years? The law of Moses says that no Hebrew can serve for more than six years. In the seventh year a Hebrew slave must go free."

"And who is there to enforce the law of Moses?"

replied the slave bitterly. "Unless one of my relatives ransoms me with a large sum of money, I shall be a slave until the end of my life."

As Jeremiah spoke to the slave, a procession passed by led by priests. The prophet said good-bye to the slave, and followed the procession.

The priests led the procession through the gate in the wall. They descended into the valley of Hinnom below the city wall.

The priests offered an animal sacrifice to the bright sun calling it a god. Then they built another fire. The prophet was horrified to see the priests thrust a human being into the fire as a burnt-offering unto the idol Baal.

"Woe unto Jerusalem!" cried Jeremiah. "God will surely punish Jerusalem because of its sins!"

3. JEREMIAH'S WARNING

The word of God came to Jeremiah to warn Jerusalem that it would be destroyed because the people had been wicked.

The prophet went to a pottery shop and bought a large earthen piece of pottery. He placed the earthen pot on his head and walked toward the city gate.

"Follow me, men of Jerusalem," shouted the prophet. "Hear the word of the Lord."

A large crowd gathered. They followed Jeremiah wondering what his message was.

The prophet walked through the gate of the city, and descended into the valley of Hinnom. It was here that a human being had been sacrificed to Baal.

"Hear, O king of Judah and men of Jerusalem," said Jeremiah. "Because you have worshiped idols, and made slaves of your brothers, and shed innocent blood, God will punish you. This valley will be called not Hinnom, but the valley of slaughter. The enemy will come and destroy Jerusalem and the royal family, and lead the people into exile!"

The prophet then lifted the earthen pottery and hurled it to the ground. It broke into a thousand pieces.

"Thus shall Judah be destroyed because of your sins!" called out the prophet.

"Arrest him!" shouted one of the king's officers. "He is guilty of treason!"

Several soldiers seized the prophet who made no attempt to escape.

"Place him in the stocks," ordered the officer.

Jeremiah's hands and feet were bound, and he was tied to the stocks in the open square.

The prophet remained in the stocks for several days. His pupil, Baruch, brought him food.

The crowds passing by jeered the prophet.

"Traitor!" they shouted. "He wants our city destroyed!"

"I want God to bless Jerusalem," replied the prophet. "But He will curse it and not bless it unless we change our wicked ways."

Meanwhile, King Jehoiakim had not yet decided what to do with Jeremiah.

"He deserves to die," said the king. "He is guilty of treason!"

Ahikam, one of the king's advisers, turned to the king and said, "Permit me, my lord, to say a word in defense of Jeremiah. When your father, King Josiah, ruled in Jerusalem, we found a book in which were written the laws of Moses. The book warned us that God would punish us if we did not obey His laws. Your father ordered us to change our evil ways and to carry out these laws. That is what Jeremiah has asked us to do. He has done nothing wrong."

"But he said that God would destroy me," replied the king. "He said our city would become a heap of ruins."

"There were prophets before him," said Ahikam. "No king ever harmed a man of God."

When the king saw that many of the officers and *Kohanim* agreed with Ahikam, he ordered the soldiers to release Jeremiah.

It was not a minute too soon.

Mobs had gathered and were shouting, "Death to the traitor! Stone him! Stone him!"

The soldiers quickly released Jeremiah who, unafraid, calmly returned to his home.

4. THE SCROLL

Although Jeremiah had almost lost his life, he continued to tell the people that there could be no peace unless they changed their ways.

"Babylon will come and destroy Jerusalem because of its sins," he warned.

Babylon was now the strongest nation in the world. It

had defeated mighty Assyria. Would it not be Judah's turn next?

The word of God came to Jeremiah saying, "Write down all that I have spoken to you concerning Judah and Jerusalem. Maybe the king and the people will change their ways and obey My laws. Then I will pardon their sins, and all will be well."

Jeremiah called Baruch, the scribe, who wrote down on a scroll all that the prophet told him.

"Take the scroll and read it to the people who gather in the Temple," said Jeremiah to Baruch.

Baruch did as Jeremiah had asked. The people listened to the words of the prophet.

Then Ahikam's nephew came to the princes and said, "I have just heard Baruch, the pupil of Jeremiah, read a scroll before the people. These are surely the words of the living God. Why do we not hearken to the voice of the prophet? Let us change our ways and maybe God will pardon us."

"Bring Baruch here," said the princes. "We, too, would like to know what the prophet has written."

When Baruch came to the chamber of the princes, they said, "Sit down and read from the scroll."

The princes heard the words of the scroll and trembled.

"How was this book written?" asked the princes.

"Jeremiah told me what to write, and I wrote it down with ink in this book," answered Baruch.

"We must tell the king about this scroll," said the princes,

"Well do I remember the day", said Ahikam, "when the *Kohen Gadol* found the book of Moses in the Temple. He gave it to my father to bring to the king. The king listened to the words in the book of Moses. He removed the idols from the land, and obeyed the laws of God. If only King Jehoiakim listened to the words in Jeremiah's book!"

Turning to Baruch who stood nearby, Ahikam whispered, "Return to Jeremiah, and both of you hide. The king may try to put you to death!"

When the princes told King Jehoiakim about the scroll, he said, "Bring it to me."

After three or four columns had been read, the king grew furious.

"Is not Jeremiah the man whom we wanted to put to death? Why did we allow him to escape? He is no prophet—he is a traitor! Destroy the scroll! I do not wish to hear any more!"

Ahikam turned to the king saying, "I plead with you, my lord. Do not destroy the scroll. Did not David listen to the words of Samuel and Nathan? Did not Hezekiah listen to the words of Isaiah? A prophet's words are holy."

The king motioned to the officer to read on.

The officer read:

> "The sin of Judah is written
>   With a pen of iron, and with the point of a
>   diamond.
>   I will scatter them as with an east wind
>   Before the enemy."

"Enough!" cried the king.

Rising angrily from his throne, the king seized a knife and slashed the scroll. He threw the scroll into the fire in the fireplace and watched it burn.

"Arrest Jeremiah and his servant," he shouted, "and put them to death!"

Jeremiah and Baruch had already escaped and could not be found.

The prophet's words soon came true. Babylonia defeated Egypt and then turned toward Judah.

King Jehoiakim died of illness while the Babylonian army was on the march. His son, afraid to resist, surrendered after a brief struggle.

The Babylonian army, under King Nebuchadnezzar, exiled the new king and thousands of the nobles and citizens of Jerusalem.

The city, however, was spared. The people sadly returned to their work.

"It is not yet too late," said Jeremiah after the surrender to Babylon. "Obey the words of God and Judah will be saved!"

EXERCISES

I. Answer each question in a complete sentence. (Review sections 1 and 2, pages 241 to 244.)
   1. What did Jeremiah say to those who believed that Jerusalem would never fall?
   2. Why were the prisoners placed in the stocks by the king's officers?

3. Why was the farmer forced to become a slave?
4. According to the law of Moses, how long may a Hebrew serve his master?
5. What did Jeremiah see in the valley of Hinnom?

II. Arrange in the order in which these events happened. (Review section 3, pages 244 to 246.)

1. Jeremiah was allowed to go free.
2. The prophet walked with an earthen pot on his head to the valley of Hinnom.
3. Jeremiah was arrested and placed in the stocks.
4. Ahikam pleaded with the king not to kill Jeremiah.
5. Jeremiah broke the earthen pot and said, "Thus shall Jerusaiem be destroyed!"

III. Match. (Review section 4, pages 246 to 249.)

Column A	Column B
Ahikam	1. Read scroll to people
Baruch	2. King of Babylon
Jehoiakim	3. Warned that Jerusalem would fall
Jeremiah	4. Burned the scroll
Nebuchadnezzar	5. Warned prophet to hide

IV. Questions for discussion:

1. Why did Jeremiah condemn the king and the people of Judah?
2. Compare Isaiah and Jeremiah.

THINGS TO DO

1. *Scroll*—The book prepared by Jeremiah and Baruch is called a *Megillah*—a scroll or roll. Construct a "Scroll of the

Prophets." Include quotations from the teachings of Isaiah and Jeremiah.

2. *Dramatization*—Act out the story of Jeremiah. Suggested scenes: a. The prisoners in the stocks; b. The slave; c. In the valley of Hinnom; d. The arrest of Jeremiah; e. The scroll.

3. *Pillory and Stocks*—Construct a wooden model of a pillory and stocks.

A SCRAMBLED PUZZLE

Unscramble the following names. What do they all have in common?

1. LEUMAS
2. HANTAN
3. HAJILE
4. HASILE
5. NOJAH
6. HAISAI
7. HAIMEJER

CHAPTER XXIII

DESTRUCTION
AND NEW HOPE

1. "FREE THE SLAVES"

JEHOIAKIM'S brother was placed by the king of Babylon on the throne of Jerusalem. The new king was named Zedekiah.

Zedekiah called his advisers and asked, "How shall I govern the Jewish people?"

Ahikam, the officer who had saved Jeremiah's life, replied, "Let us ask the prophet for his advice. He will tell us the word of God."

When Jeremiah was called before King Zedekiah, he said, "My lord, obey the words of God and you have nothing to fear. Babylon will treat you kindly. Do not try to rebel."

"What about the captives in Babylon? How can we arrange for their return?"

"Let them build houses, and plant vineyards and work for the welfare of the cities of Babylon in which they dwell. Seventy years will pass by before the captives return."

"What must I do to obtain God's blessing?" asked King Zedekiah.

"Free the slaves!" replied Jeremiah. "Moses commanded us in the Torah to free our Hebrew servants after six years. Let all who have served more than six years be freed."

"The slaves will be freed!" promised Zedekiah.

The king sent messengers to all the cities of Judah to declare the words of Moses, "Proclaim liberty throughout all the land unto all the inhabitants thereof."

The princes of Judah gathered in the Temple and drew up a covenant.

"We will free our Hebrew slaves who have served more than six years," they agreed.

Jeremiah was overjoyed. Perhaps the new king would follow in the footsteps of his father, the righteous King Josiah. Maybe God would bless the Jews as in the days of King David and King Hezekiah.

But things soon changed.

"Jeremiah is a traitor," declared many of the nobles. "He tells us to forget our brothers who have been taken captive to Babylon. Besides, he wants us to free our slaves. Did we not pay good money for them on the market?"

When the time came for freeing the slaves the nobles protested to the king.

Poor Zedekiah did not know in which direction to turn. Ahikam and his son, Gedaliah, urged the king to follow Jeremiah's advice.

"How can I make enemies of all my nobles?" thought

Zedekiah. "It is better not to enforce our agreement about the slaves. Let each family try to redeem its own relatives."

A few nobles had given their slaves freedom. But as soon as they saw that the agreement would not be carried out, they forced the slaves to return.

And the word of God came to Jeremiah saying, "Because Zedekiah and the nobles have broken their promise, I shall deliver them into the hands of their enemies. Babylon will return to this city and burn it with fire, and Judah shall become a heap of ruins."

2. REBELLION AGAINST BABYLON

Nine years after Zedekiah had become king, he rebelled against Nebuchadnezzar, the king of Babylon.

Jeremiah warned against the rebellion. He took a yoke which is placed around the neck of an ox to force it to plow.

"Bring your necks under the yoke of the king of Babylon. Serve him and you will live. Rebel against him and you will die."

One of the false prophets took the wooden yoke from Jeremiah and broke it in two.

"Thus will the Lord break the yoke of Babylon," declared the false prophet. "In two more years our captives will return."

"Would that it could be so!" replied Jeremiah. "But if the king rebels against Babylon, instead of a yoke of wood Judah will wear a yoke of iron."

Jeremiah's words soon came true. Nebuchadnezzar sent

a large army against Judah and besieged all of the large cities.

Jerusalem was in great distress. People hungered for food and thirsted for water. Jeremiah knew that Zedekiah must soon surrender.

"Surrender and live," called out Jeremiah in the streets of Jerusalem.

"This man makes the people lose heart," complained the princes. "Let us arrest him."

King Zedekiah did not want to harm the prophet, but out of fear of the princes, he placed Jeremiah under guard in the court of the palace.

Jeremiah had given up hope for Jerusalem, but he knew that some day Jerusalem would be rebuilt.

"I must encourage those who still believe in God," thought Jeremiah. "Jerusalem will be destroyed, but some day the exiles will return."

The word of God came to Jeremiah saying, "Redeem the field belonging to your cousin in your native village of Anathoth."

Jeremiah's cousin came to see the prophet.

"Redeem my field, Jeremiah," said his cousin. "I must sell to pay my debts. It is better that you should buy it than for me to sell to a stranger."

Jeremiah called the men in the court to serve as witnesses. He signed the bill of sale, and weighed out seventeen shekels of silver on the scales.

"You are witnesses," said the prophet, "that I have bought the field."

"We are witnesses," they replied.

The prophet handed the bill of sale to Baruch.

"Keep this in a safe place," said Jeremiah.

"Why do you buy a field at a time when the country is being destroyed by the enemy?" asked one of the men who had witnessed the sale. "Of what value is a field in a ruined country?"

"God will gather all the exiles and bring them back to Judah. And they will be God's people for they will serve God with a pure heart. Fields will again be bought in this land. Men will buy fields in Jerusalem, in the cities of Judah, in the hill-country, in the south and in the north. God will plant the exiles in their own land where they will dwell in safety."

The prophet of sorrow had become a prophet of hope. Some day the city of Jerusalem would be rebuilt, and the exiles would return to their own land!

3. JEREMIAH A PRISONER

King Zedekiah hoped that Egypt would come to his rescue. Were it not for his trust in Egypt he might never have rebelled against Babylon.

In the midst of the siege word came, "Egypt has gone up against Babylon."

Nebuchadnezzar removed his troops from Jerusalem to meet the army of Egypt. There was great rejoicing in Jerusalem. Perhaps Babylon would be defeated.

Jeremiah was allowed to go free since the enemy was no longer at the gates of the city.

The king secretly sent messengers to Jeremiah to inquire whether Jerusalem would now be free.

"There is no hope for Jerusalem," said Jeremiah. "Egypt will be defeated and Nebuchadnezzar will return to attack Judah."

Meanwhile, in the absence of the army of Babylon, the prophet decided to visit his native village of Anathoth. Some of his relatives were still in the village. The prophet also wanted to inspect his house and the new field that he had bought.

As he left Jerusalem he was stopped by the guard.

"You are a spy," said the soldiers. "You wish to escape to the camp of the Babylonians."

"I am no spy," replied Jeremiah. "I shall remain with my people in Jerusalem until the bitter end. I am going to visit my home in the village of Anathoth."

"You lie! You are a spy!" said the soldiers.

Jeremiah was brought to the princes who angrily said, "This is the man who urged us to surrender. Let us throw him into the pit."

The prophet was thrown into a pit in the court of the guards. There was no water in the pit but mire. The prophet sank in the mud up to his neck.

"Help! Help!" cried Jeremiah, for he could not remain alive long in the mire of the pit.

The prophet would surely have died were it not for the help of a negro soldier, named Ebed-melech. When Ebed-melech heard that the princes had thrown Jeremiah into the pit he hurried to King Zedekiah.

"My lord," said the negro officer, "the princes have done an evil thing. Jeremiah has not been a spy or a traitor. He only warned that Babylon would attack and his warning has come true. Do not allow the princes to shed innocent blood, for Jeremiah will surely die in the pit."

"You are right," replied the king. "Take thirty soldiers with you and rescue Jeremiah."

Ebed-melech found some ropes and rags, then led the soldiers to the pit into which Jeremiah had been thrown.

"Jeremiah! Jeremiah!" called the negro officer. "Do you hear me?"

From the pit came a weak voice, "Help! Help!"

"I shall lower these rags by means of ropes," said Ebed-melech. "Place the worn rags under your arms, and we will draw you out of the pit."

The rags were lowered. Jeremiah hardly had enough strength to place the rags under his arms.

"Are you ready?" called Ebed-melech.

"Ready," Jeremiah weakly replied.

"Pull!" commanded the negro officer.

The soldiers pulled at the rope until Jeremiah was raised from the pit.

Jeremiah was again placed under guard in the court of the king. There he remained until the end of the siege.

4. THE FALL OF JERUSALEM

Nebuchadnezzar defeated Egypt and then returned to the siege of Jerusalem. The siege lasted, in all, for a year and a half.

At last the Babylonian soldiers placed a mound against the wall, and made a breach in the wall.

"Let us flee for our lives," said King Zedekiah.

The king and the royal family fled toward the plain of the Jordan River. The soldiers of Babylon pursued after the king and overtook him near Jericho.

Zedekiah was brought to King Nebuchadnezzar. Like Samson he was blinded, and was then brought in chains to Babylon.

Nebuchadnezzar ransacked the Temple. All of the precious objects were taken to Babylon.

Then, on the ninth day of the month of Av in the year 586 B.C.E., the Babylonians set fire to the entire city. The Temple, built almost 400 years before by King Solomon, went up in flames.

The palace and all the houses of Jerusalem were burned to the ground. Jerusalem, the great capital of King David, lay in ruins!

Jeremiah was taken prisoner, but the king of Babylon warned the soldiers not to harm him in any way.

"You may come with us to Babylon," said the captain to Jeremiah, "and we shall treat you kindly. But if you wish to stay in Judah, you are free to do so."

"I shall stay in Judah," replied Jeremiah.

The prophet sadly watched the flames as they rose toward the sky. Tears welled up in his eyes.

"Judah has gone into exile," wept the prophet. "Her children are captive. How sad is the city that was once full of rejoicing! Gone are her splendor and her glory!"

Meanwhile, the exiles were forced to march to Babylon. When they reached the rivers of Babylon they sat down to rest.

"Sing us some of the songs of Zion," mocked the Babylonian soldiers.

The exiles placed their harps on the willow trees and refused to play.

"How shall we sing the Lord's song in a strange land?" they asked.

Instead the exiles took an oath:

"If I forget thee, O Jerusalem,
Let my right hand forget her skill.
Let my tongue cleave to the roof of my mouth,
If I remember thee not;
If I set not Jerusalem
Above my chiefest joy."

5. NEW HOPE

The king of Babylon had allowed the poorest of the land to remain in Judah.

"We must not lose hope," Jeremiah taught the people. "God will some day bring back the exiles to rebuild the land."

One day the prophet dreamed a strange dream. He dreamed that when the exiles passed Rachel's tomb they heard the sound of weeping.

"Mother Rachel is weeping for her children," said the exiles.

Before the throne of God went Rachel. The tears rolled down her cheek. None could console her.

"Is this the reward of the Hebrew people for the good deeds of Abraham, Isaac and Jacob?" wept Rachel. "Is this the fate of the descendants of Judah and Benjamin, of Moses and Aaron, of the great leaders and prophets?"

Then was heard the voice of God:

> "Refrain thy voice from weeping,
>   And thine eyes from tears;
>   For thy work shall be rewarded, saith the
>   Lord;
>   And they shall come back from the land of
>   the enemy.
>   And there is hope for thy future, saith the
>   Lord;
>   And thy children shall return to their own
>   border."

Jeremiah awoke from his sleep. It was only a dream. But for the first time in many years his sleep had been sweet.

Day and night Jeremiah repeated these words to all: "There is hope for our future. Our children will return to their own land!"

Meanwhile, the king of Babylon had made Gedaliah governor over the poor people who remained in Judah.

Gedaliah was a wise and good man who had warned Zedekiah to obey the words of Jeremiah. His father, Ahikam, had been Jeremiah's friend and had saved his life when the prophet was placed in the stocks.

Jeremiah was very happy to hear that Gedaliah was made governor.

But, alas, outlaws roamed through the ruined cities of Judah. Gedaliah was soon slain.

The people, in terror, fled for their lives to Egypt.

"Let us remain in Judah," pleaded Jeremiah. "Do not lose hope!"

The people, however, forced Jeremiah to go along with them to Egypt. There he lived for the rest of his life, urging the Jewish people to worship God with pure hearts.

Wherever Jews had been exiled they repeated the words of the prophet, "Do not lose hope! Do not lose hope!"

They sang a new song of hope. And their dreams were not in vain. Many of the captives lived to see the day when Cyrus the Great conquered Babylon, and proclaimed that the exiles could return to rebuild their land and their Temple.

Jeremiah's prophecy of hope had come true!

EXERCISES

   I. Who? (Review section 1, pages 252 to 254.)
      1. Who was the new king?
      2. Who advised the king to consult Jeremiah?
      3. Who warned the king to free the slaves?
      4. Who gathered in the Temple and drew up an agreement to free the slaves?
      5. Who protested that Jeremiah was a traitor?

II. Complete each sentence. (Review section 2, pages 254 to 256.)

Baruch, false prophet, Jeremiah, Nebuchadnezzer, Zedekiah

1. Zedekiah rebelled against _____.
2. The _____ said that God would break the yoke of Babylon.
3. _____ placed Jeremiah under guard.
4. _____ bought his cousin's field as a sign that the fields of Judah would some day be very valuable.
5. The bill of sale was given to _____.

III. Who said to whom? (Review section 3, pages 256 to 258.)

1. "Egypt will be defeated and Nebuchadnezzar will return to attack Judah."
2. "You are a spy. You wish to escape to the camp of the Babylonians."
3. "I am no spy. I am going to visit my home in the village of Anathoth."
4. "Do not allow the princes to shed innocent blood, for Jeremiah will surely die in the pit."
5. "Take thirty soldiers with you and rescue Jeremiah."
6. "Place the worn rags under your arms, and we will draw you out of the pit."

IV. True or false? (Review sections 4 and 5, pages 258 to 262.)

1. Zedekiah was captured by the Babylonians and treated kindly.
2. The Temple burned on the 9th of Av.
3. Jeremiah went with the exiles to Babylon.
4. The exiles swore, "If I forget thee, O Jerusalem, let my right hand forget her skill."

5. Jeremiah dreamed that God told Mother Rachel not to weep because the exiles would return.
6. Gedaliah remained governor of Judah for many years.
7. Jeremiah's prophecy of hope came true when Cyrus the Great permitted the exiles to return to their land.

V. Questions for discussion:
1. "Zedekiah was a weak king who could not decide what to do." Show how this is true.
2. In what ways did Jeremiah try to give the people new hope?

REVIEW QUESTIONS

for Units Five and Six (pages 221 to 264)

1. Discuss the main message of each of the following prophets: Elijah, Jonah, Isaiah, Jeremiah.
2. Mention one important act of each of the following kings: Rehoboam, Jereboam, Ahab, Hezekiah, Jehoikim, Zedekiah.
3. "The prophets are more important in Jewish history than the kings." Why is this true?
4. Identify each of the following: Ahijah, Jezebel, Naboth, Elisha, Sennacherib, Baruch, Ahikam, Ebedmelech, Nebuchadnezzar, Cyrus the Great.
5. Where?

   a. Where did Jereboam and the ten tribes of Israel rebel against Rehoboam?

   b. Where did Elijah hear the "still small voice"?

   c. Where was the capital of the ten tribes of Israel?

   d. Where did Jonah proclaim that the city would be destroyed?

e. Where was Isaiah when he saw a vision of the angels singing, "Holy, holy, holy is the Lord, God of hosts."?

f. Where, according to the legend, did the lost ten tribes go?

g. Where did Jeremiah see the people offer a sacrifice to Baal?

h. Where was the capital of Judah?

i. Where were the exiles taken by Nebuchadnezzar?

j. Where did Jeremiah live after Gedaliah was slain?

TEST

for Units Five and Six

I. Why? (30 points)

1. Why did the people complain to Solomon's son?
2. Why did Jeroboam set up calves as idols in Israel?
3. Why was Elijah angry at Ahab?
4. Why did Jonah run away when he was told by God to go to Nineveh?
5. Why is Isaiah called "the prophet of peace"?
6. Why did Jeremiah break an earthen pot in the valley of Hinnom?

II. Mention two great teachings of the prophets. (8 points)

III. What is my name? (24 points)

1. I tore my garment into 12 parts and gave Jereboam ten, as a sign that the ten tribes of Israel would rebel.
2. I was a wicked queeen. I set up temples to Baal, and put honest people to death when I wanted their fields.

3. I learned the lesson that God pardons sins if the sinner repents. My story is read on Yom Kippur.
4. I built the Siloam Tunnel to provide water for Jerusalem. In my day Judah was saved from Sennacherib, the king of Assyria.
5. I was the last king of Judah. I rebelled against Babylon.
6. I was a negro officer who saved the life of Jeremiah by drawing him up from the pit.

IV. Complete each sentence by filling in the name of the place. (20 points)

1. The capital of the ten tribes of Israel in the days of Ahab was _____.
2. Elijah heard the "still small voice" at Mount _____.
3. Jonah proclaimed, "In forty more days _____ will be destroyed."
4. The children of the lost ten tribes are waiting in the land of _____ for all exiles to return to Israel.
5. "If I forget thee, O _____, let my right hand forget her skill."

V. Match. (18 points)

Column A	Column B
Ahikam	1. Passover guest
Cyrus	2. Wept for exiles
Elijah	3. Permitted exiles to return
Isaiah	4. Owner of vineyard
Naboth	5. Saved life of Jeremiah
Rachel	6. Swords into plowshares

Guide to Pronunciation

KEY

ärm	thēre	nŏt
hăt	thêy	môre
câre	înk	rūle
āte	īce	ŭp
ēat	ĭll	fûr
ĕnd	ōld	ś as in "waś"

Glossary

Aâr′on

A-bǐ′me-lĕch ("ch" as in "Jericho")

A-bǐsh′a-ī

Ăb′ner

Ā′bra-hăm

Ăb′sa-lŏm

Ā′chăn ("ch" as in "Jericho")

A-dō-nī′jah

Ā′hăb

A-hăś-u-ē′rus

Ā′hăz

A-hī′jah

A-hī′kam

A-hī′tho-phel

Aī

Aī′ja-lon

Ak′a-ba

Äl S′fät Yäm Kǐn-nē′rĕt

A-măl′e-kīte

Ăm′mon-īte

Ăm′non

Ā′năth-ŏth

ä-rôn′kô′dĕsh

Ăsh′er

Ăs-syr′i-a

Äv

Ä-vǐ′nū Mäl-kê′-nū

267

Bā'ăl

Băb'y-lŏn

Bā'răk

Bā'rūch

Băth'she-ba

Bē'er-shē'ba

Bĕth' Ĕl

Bĕth'le-hĕm

Bĕth'-shăn

Bĭk-kū-rīm'

Bō'ăz

brĭth

Cā'naan

Cär'mĕl

Chäd Gäd-yä' (guttural "ch")

Chăg Nĕch-mäd' (guttural "ch")

chä-lū-tzīm' (guttural "ch")

chä-zäk' vē-ē-mätz' (guttural "ch")

Chĭl'-ĭ-on ("ch" as in "Jericho")

Cy'-rus

Dā'gon

Da-măs'cus

Dā'vĭd

Dĕb'o-rah

De-lī'lah

Ē'bed-me-lĕch ("ch" as in "Jericho")

Êin-hăr'od

Ē'lăth

Ĕl-e-ā'zar

Ê-lee-yä'hū Hä-Nä-vî'

Ē'lī

E-lī'ăb

E-lī'jah

E-lĭm'e-lĕch ("ch" as in "Jericho")

E-lī'sha

Ĕl-kā'nah

Ē'phra-ĭm

Ẽ'rĕtz Yĭs-rä-el'

Ē'sau

Eu-phrā'tēṡ

Găd

Găl'ĭl-ee

Găth

Gā'za

Gē'ba

Gĕd-a-lī'ah

Ge-rī'zĭm

Gĭb'e-on

Gĭd'e-on

Gī'hon

Gĭl-bō'a

Gĭl'e-ăd

Gĭl'găl

Go-lī'ăth

Gō'shen

Hā'gar

Häg-gä-däh'

Hä-Gĭl-a-dî'

Hăn'nah

Hä-Tĭsh-bî'

Hä-Yär-děn'

Hē'bron

Hĕz-e-kī'ah

Hĭn-nêh'mäh tôv

Hĭn'nōm

Hī'ram

Hū'sha-ī

Ĭch'a-bŏd ("ch" as in "Jericho")

Ī'ṡaac

Ī-ṡāi'ah

Ish-bō'sheth

Iṡ'ra-el

Ĭs'sa-char ("ch" as in "Jericho")

Jā'besh

Jā'cob

Jā'ĕl

Jăf'-fa

Je-hoi'a-kĭm

Jē'hū

Jĕr-e-bō'am

Jĕr-e-mī'ah

Jĕr'i-chō

Je-rū'sa-lem

Jĕs'se

Jĕz'e-bĕl

Jĕz're-ĕl

Jō'ăb

Jō'nah

Jŏn'a-than

Jôr'dan

Jō'ṡeph

Jōsh'u-a

Jō-sī'ah

Jō'tham

Jū'dah

Kä-dôsh'

Kĭn-nē'rĕt

Kĭsh

Kī'shon

Kô-hä-nîm'

Kô-hĕn'

Kô-hĕn' Gä-döl'

Kôs Ê-lee-yä'-hū

Lĕb'a-non

Lē'vīte

Le-wit'tĕs

Mä-hĕr'shä-läl'

Mäh'lŏn

Ma-năs'seh

Mä-tzäh'

Mĕd-i-ter-rā'nē-an

Me-gĭl-läh'

Me-nô-rah'

Mes-sī'ah

Mī'chal ("ch" as in "Jericho")

Mĭd'ĭ-ăn

Mĭz-môr' L'Dä-vîd'

Mĭz'pah

Mō'ăb

Mō′sės

Rūth

Nā′bŏth
Nā′hăsh
Nāō′mî
Năph′ta-lī
Nā′than
Năz′a-rīte
Nē′bō
Nĕb-u-chăd-nĕz′zar ("ch" as in
  "Jericho")
nĕr tä-mîd′
Nĭn′e-veh

Ō′bed
Ô′mer
Ō′phîr
Ôr′päh

Pe-nîn′nah
Phā′raōh
Phĭ-lĭs′tĭnes
Phĭn′ē-as
Phoe-nĭ′-cia
Pū-rim′

Rā′chel
Rā′hăb
Rā′mah
Re-bĕc′ca
Rĕ-ho-bō′am
Reū′ben
Rôsh Hä-Shä-näh′

Sä-lêy′nū
Sa-mā′ri-a
Säm-bät′yôn
Săm′son
Săm′u-el
Saul (rhymes with "ball")
Se-năch′er-ib ("ch" as in
  "Jericho")
Shä-vū-ôt′
She-är′-yä-shūv′
Shē′ba
Shē′chem ("ch" as in "Jericho")
shĭb′bo-leth
Shî′lōh
Shîr Hä-mä-ä-lôt′
shô-fär′
Sĭd-dūr′
Sĭ-lō′am
Sĭm′ē-on
Sĭ′naī
Sĭs′e-ra
S'läch Lä′nū (guttural "ch")
Sŏl′o-mon
Suk-kôt′
Syr′i-a

tăb′er-nă-cle
Tā′bor
Tär′shĭsh
Te-kō′a
Tĕl-A-vîv′

This'be

Tĭm'näh

Tĭsh'bīte

Tō'rah

Tū Bi-shvät'

Tyre (rhymes with "fire")

U-rī'ah

Văsh'tī

Weīz'mann (z pronounced "ts")

Xer'xēs̀

Yĕm'en

Yôm Kip-pur'

Zĕb'u-lun

Zĕd-e-kī'ah

Zĭk'lăg

Zĭ'on

Zĭph